SPECTRUM SERIES
PHONICS

Published 1997 McGraw-Hill Learning Materials

TABLE OF CONTENTS

Eye-hand Coordination	3
Left-to-right Progression	4
Visual Discrimination of Pictures	5
Short *A, B*	7
C, D	13
Short *E, F*	19
Review: *A, E*	23
F	24
Review: *B, C, D, F*	26
G, H	27
Short *I, J*	33
K, L	39
Review: *G, H, J, K*	43
L	44
M, N	46
Short *O, P*	52
Review: *I, O*	56
P	57
Review: *L, M, N, P*	59
Q, R	60
S, T	66
Review: *Qu, R, S, T*	72
Short *U, V*	73
Review: *U*	77
V	78

EAN

W, X	80
Y, Z	86
Review: *V, W, X, Y, Z*	92
Progress Check: Consonants	93
Progress Check: Vowels	95
Answer Key	97

INSTRUCTIONAL CONSULTANT
Mary Lou Maples, Ed.D.
Chairman of Department of Education
Huntingdon College
Montgomery, Alabama

EDITORIAL AND PRODUCTION STAFF
Series Editor: Joyce R. Rhymer; *Project Editor:* Suzanne Senn Diehm; *Production Editor:* Carole R. Hill; *Senior Designer:* Patrick J. McCarthy; *Associate Designer:* Terry D. Anderson; *Project Artist:* Gilda Braxton Edwards; *Ilustrators:* Lisy Boren, Ethel Gold

Copyright © 1998 McGraw-Hill Consumer Products.
Published by McGraw-Hill Learning Materials, an imprint of
McGraw-Hill Consumer Products.

Printed in the United States of America.

Organized for successful learning!

The SPECTRUM PHONICS SERIES builds the right skills for reading.

The program combines four important skill strands — phonics, structural analysis, vocabulary, and dictionary skills — so your students build the skills they need to become better readers.

Four types of lesson pages offer thorough, clearly focused, systematic skills practice. That means you can focus on just the skills that need work — for the whole class, a small group, or for individualized instruction.

The SPECTRUM PHONICS SERIES is easy for students to use independently.

Although phonics may be an important part of a reading program, sometimes there just isn't enough time to do it all. That's why PHONICS offers uncomplicated lessons your children can succeed with on their own.

Colorful borders capture interest, highlight essential information, and help organize lesson structure. And your children get off to a good start with concise explanations and clear directions . . . followed by sample answers that show them exactly what to do.

In addition, vocabulary has been carefully controlled so your children work with familiar words. Key pictures and key words are used consistently throughout the series to represent specific sounds. And a sound-symbol chart at the back of the text helps your students quickly recall sound-symbol relationships.

INSTRUCTION PAGE . . . The skill being covered is noted at the bottom of each student page for easy reference.

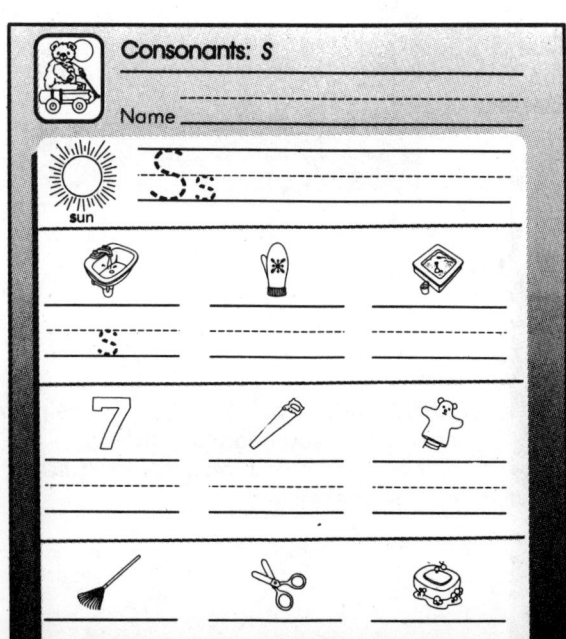

REINFORCEMENT PAGE . . . Comprehension exercises that use context as well as phonics skills to help build the connection from decoding to comprehension.

Turn page for more information.

Easy to manage

REVIEW PAGES . . . Frequent reviews emphasize skills application.

ASSESSMENT PAGES . . . Assessment pages give you helpful feedback on how your students are doing.

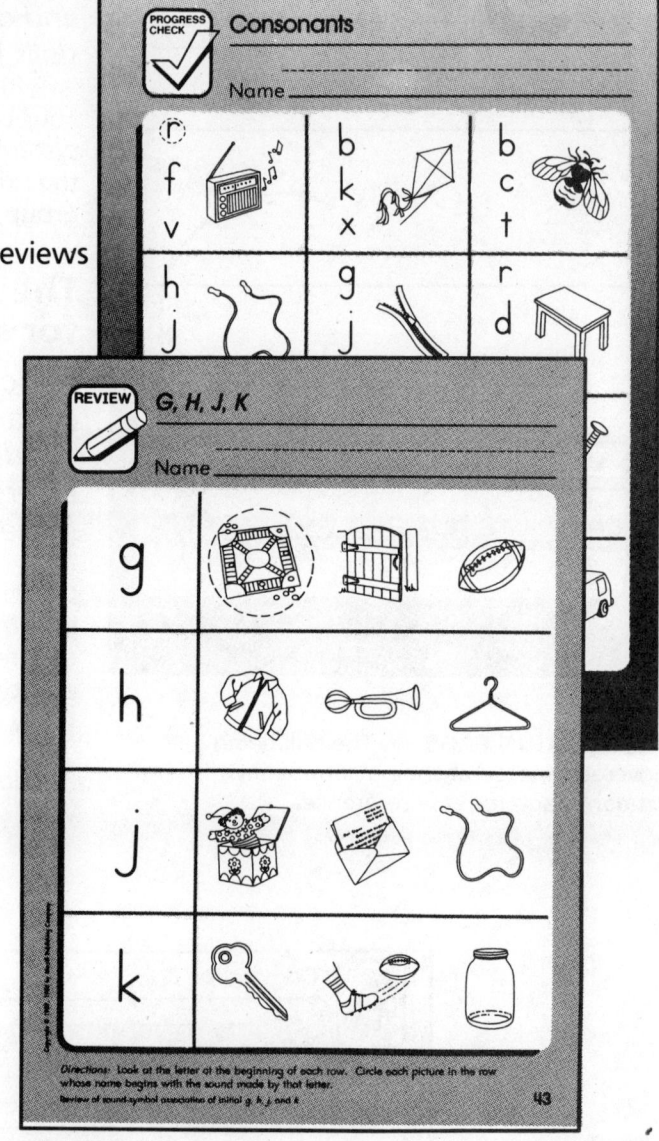

ANSWER KEY . . . Gives you the help you need when you need it — including student pages with answers for quick, easy reference.

Completing Pictures

Name _____

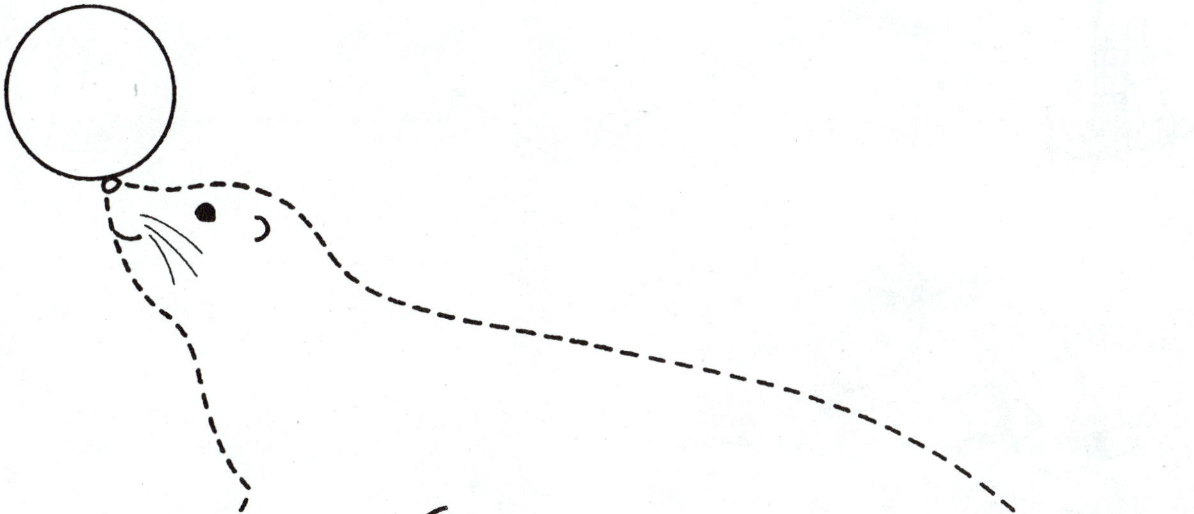

Directions: Complete each picture by tracing the dotted lines. Color each picture.

Eye-hand coordination

3

Moving from Left to Right

Name

Directions: Beginning at the black dot, trace the dotted line in each picture, moving from left to right.

Matching Pictures

Name_____

Directions: In each row, circle the picture that is the same as the first picture in the row.

Visual discrimination of pictures

5

Matching Pictures

Name _____

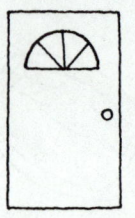 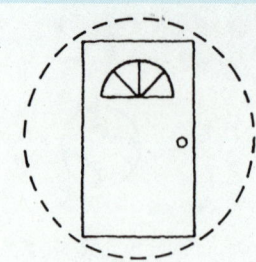  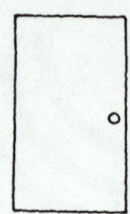

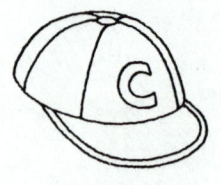  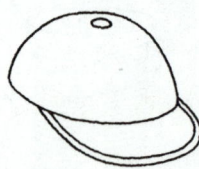 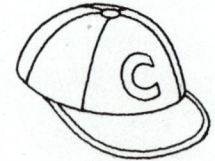

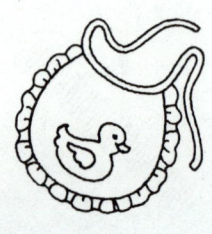 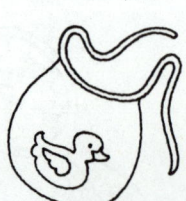  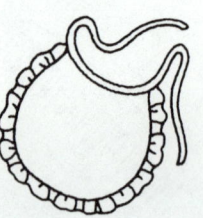

Directions: In each row, circle the picture that is the same as the first picture in the row.

Visual discrimination of pictures

Matching Letters

Name_____

| A a 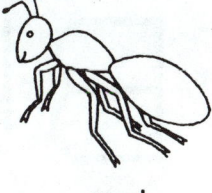 **a**nt | B b  **b**all |

A	V (A) H A
a	a o a e
B	B K T B
b	f g b b

Directions: In each row, circle the letters that are the same as the first letter in the row.

Visual discrimination of capital and lowercase *a* and *b*

Matching Letters

Name _____

Aa  **a**nt	Bb **b**all		
A	h	(a) x a	
a	A P D A		
B	t b f b		
b	B L M B		

Directions: Look at the letter at the beginning of each row. Circle the letters in that row that belong with the first letter.

Matching capital with lowercase *a* and *b*

Short A

Name _____

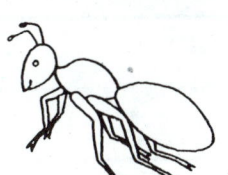 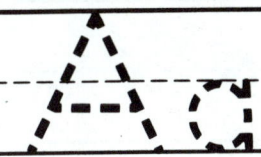

ant

  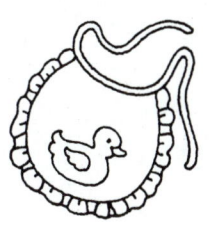 

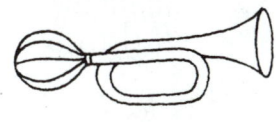   

Directions: Name the pictures. Circle each picture whose name begins with the sound you hear at the beginning of *ant*.

Auditory discrimination of initial short *a*

Short A

Name _____

f**a**n

A a

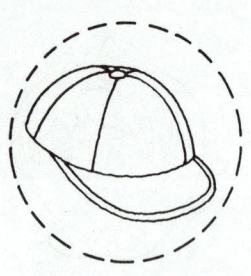  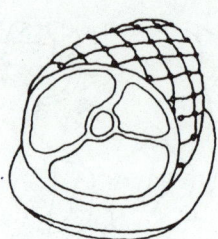 

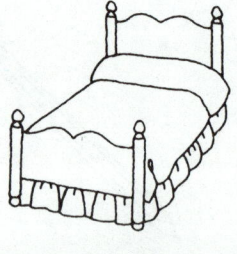   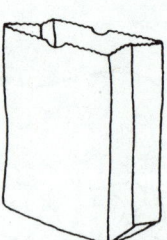

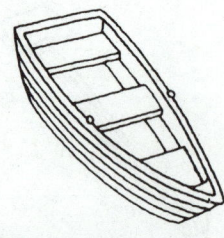 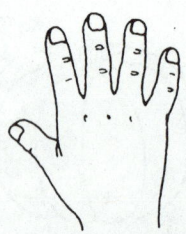 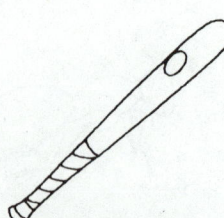 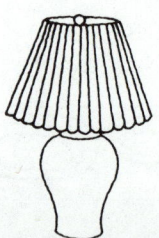

Directions: Name the pictures. Circle each picture whose name has the sound you hear in the middle of *fan*.

10

Auditory discrimination of medial short *a*

Consonants: B

Name_____

ball

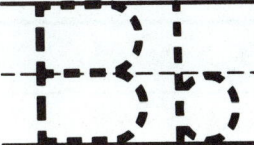

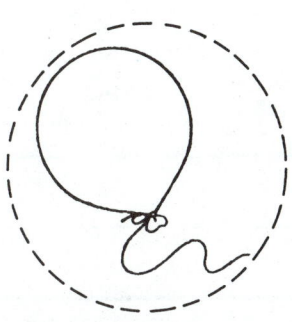 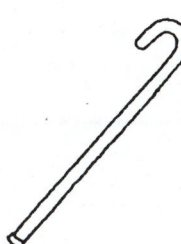  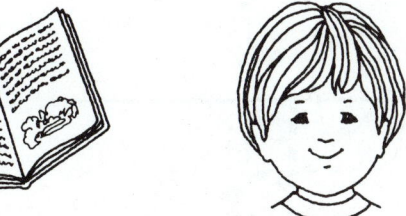

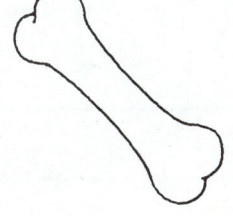  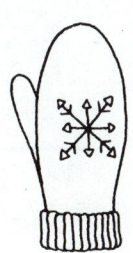 

Directions: Name the pictures. Circle each picture whose name begins with the sound you hear at the beginning of *ball*.

Auditory discrimination of initial *b*

Consonants: B

Name _____

ball

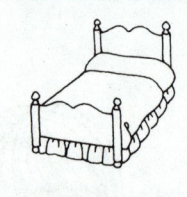

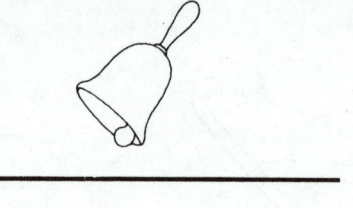

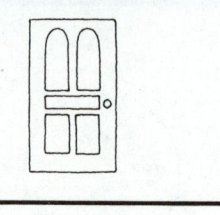

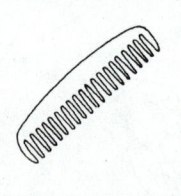

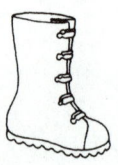

Directions: Name the pictures. Write the letter *b* below each picture whose name begins with *b*.

Sound-symbol association of initial *b*

Matching Letters

Name _____

C c car	D d dog

| C | C | G | C | O |

| c | o | c | n | c |

| D | O | D | D | B |

| d | d | h | g | d |

Directions: In each row, circle the letters that are the same as the first letter in the row.

Visual discrimination of capital and lowercase *c* and *d*

Matching Letters

Name _____

C c  **c**ar			D d 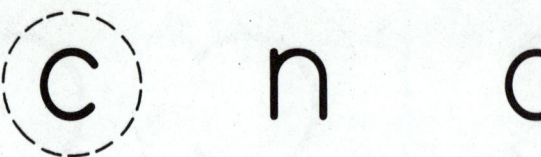 **d**og	
C	h	ⓒ	n	c
c	C	D	V	C
D	d	t	k	d
d	U	D	L	D

Directions: Look at the letter at the beginning of each row. Circle the letters in that row that belong with the first letter.

14

Matching capital with lowercase *c* and *d*

Consonants: C

Name _____

car

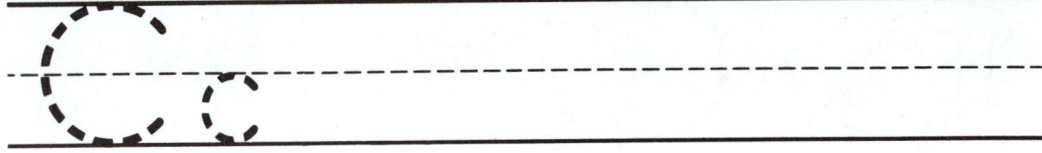

 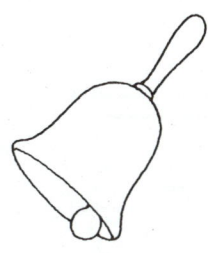 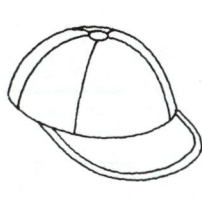 

Directions: Name the pictures. Circle each picture whose name begins with the sound you hear at the beginning of *car*.

Auditory discrimination of initial c

Consonants: C

Name _____

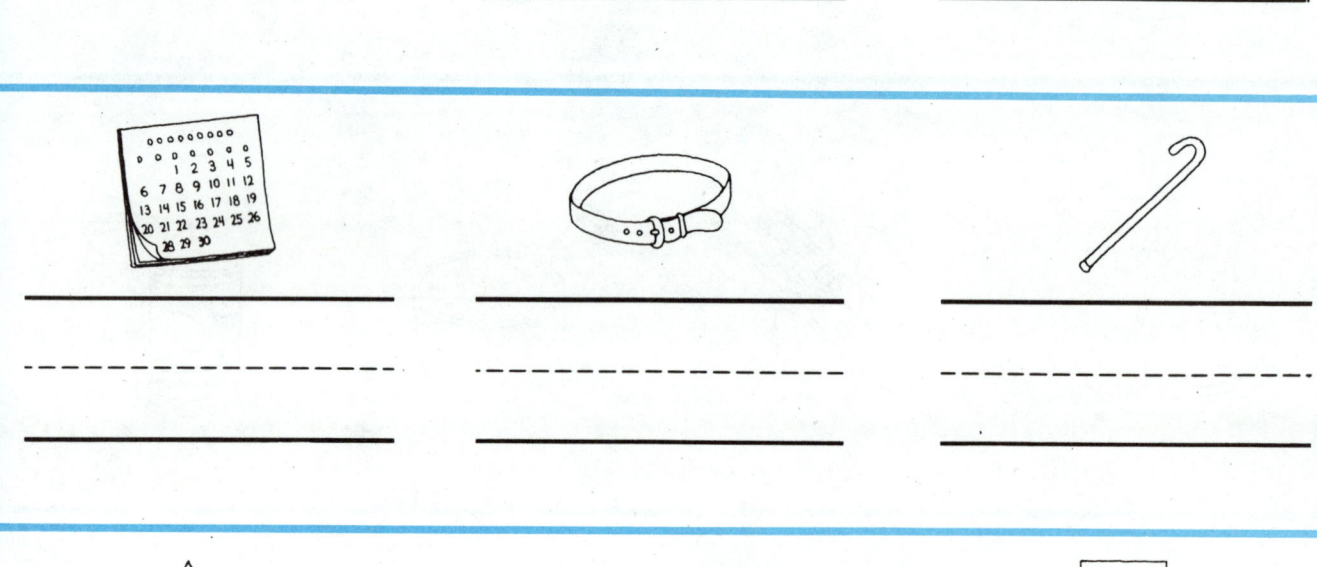

car

Directions: Name the pictures. Write the letter *c* below each picture whose name begins with *c*.

16

Sound-symbol association of initial *c*

Consonants: D

Name _____

dog

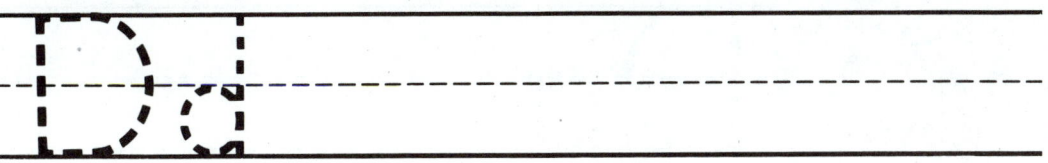

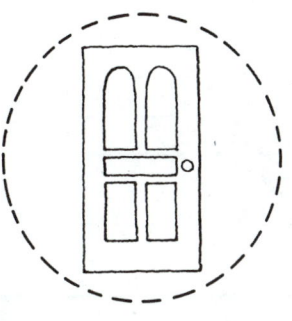   

 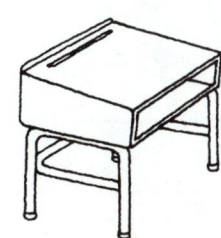 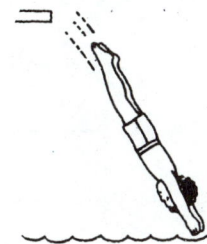 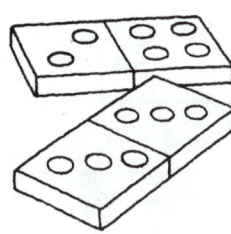

Directions: Name the pictures. Circle each picture whose name begins with the sound you hear at the beginning of *dog*.

Auditory discrimination of initial *d*

17

Consonants: *D*

Name _____

dog

Directions: Name the pictures. Write the letter *d* below each picture whose name begins with *d*.

18

Sound-symbol association of initial *d*

Matching Letters

Name _____

E e elephant			F f fish	
E	(E)	F	B	E
e	a	e	v	e
F	T	E	F	F
f	f	l	f	k

Directions: In each row, circle the letters that are the same as the first letter in the row.

Visual discrimination of capital and lowercase *e* and *f*

19

Matching Letters

Name _____

E e	F f
elephant	fish

E	e　n　e　o
e	M　E　H　E
F	f　h　l　f
f	A　F　T　F

Directions: Look at the letter at the beginning of each row. Circle the letters in that row that belong with the first letter.

20

Matching capital with lowercase *e* and *f*

Short E

Name _____

elephant

 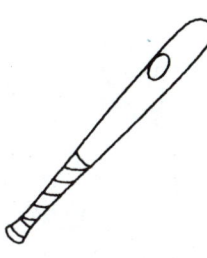  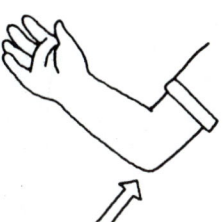

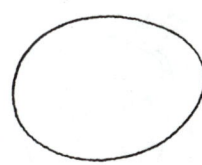   

Directions: Name the pictures. Circle each picture whose name begins with the sound you hear at the beginning of *elephant*.

Auditory discrimination of initial short *e*

Short *E*

Name _____

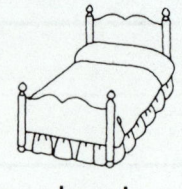
bed

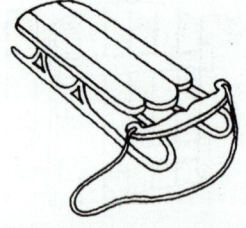
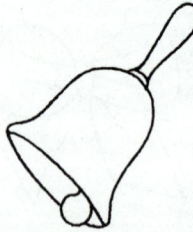
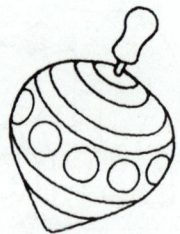
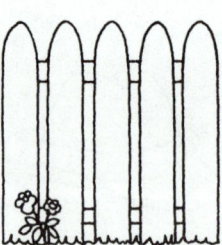

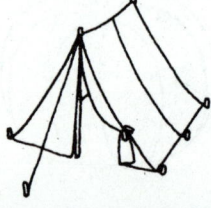

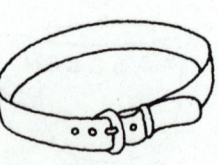

Directions: Name the pictures. Circle each picture whose name has the sound you hear in the middle of *bed*.

Auditory discrimination of medial short *e*

REVIEW

A and E

Name _____

Directions: Look at the picture at the beginning of each row. Circle each picture in the row whose name begins with the same sound as the first picture.

 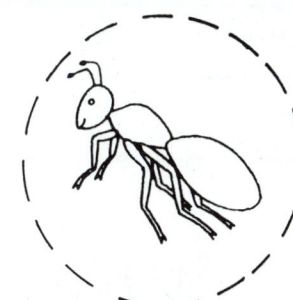  

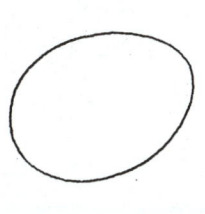  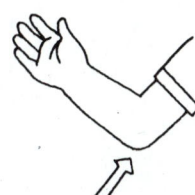 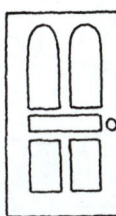

Directions: Look at the picture at the beginning of each row. Circle each picture in the row whose name has the same middle sound as the first picture.

 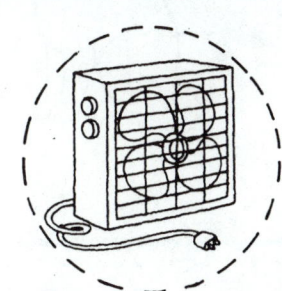 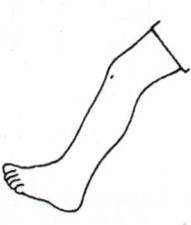 

Review of auditory discrimination of short *a* and short *e* in initial and medial positions

Consonants: F

Name _____

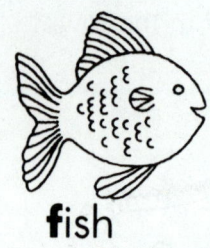 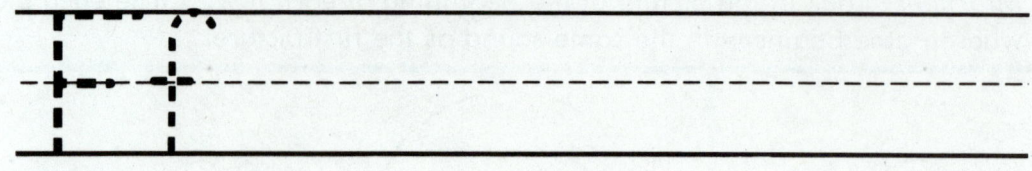

fish

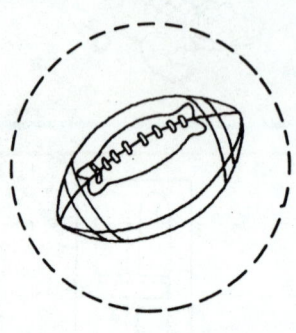   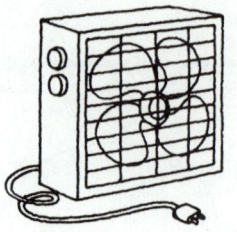

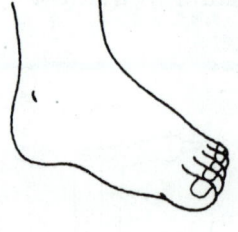   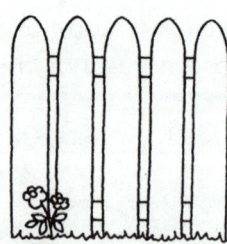

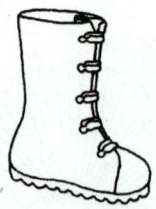  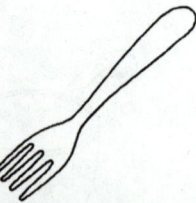 

Directions: Name the pictures. Circle each picture whose name begins with the sound you hear at the beginning of *fish*.

Auditory discrimination of initial *f*

Consonants: F

Name _____

fish

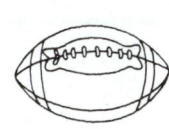

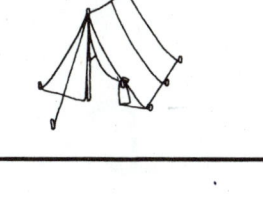

Directions: Name the pictures. Write the letter *f* below each picture whose name begins with *f*.

Sound-symbol association of initial *f*

25

REVIEW: B, C, D, F

Name _____

b	bear	doll	dive
c	bat	cow	can
d	doctor	boot	desk
f	goat	fence	fork

Directions: Look at the letter at the beginning of each row. Circle each picture in the row whose name begins with the sound made by that letter.

Review of sound-symbol association of initial b, c, d, and f

Matching Letters

Name _____

G g goat	H h horse
G	C (G) F G
g	g y g j
H	H L I H
h	d h h l

Directions: In each row, circle the letters that are the same as the first letter in the row.

Visual discrimination of capital and lowercase *g* and *h*

27

Matching Letters

Name _____

G g  **g**oat	H h  **h**orse
G	 d g y
g	Q G S G
H	k l h h
h	H A X H

Directions: Look at the letter at the beginning of each row. Circle the letters in that row that belong with the first letter.

Matching capital with lowercase *g* and *h*

Consonants: G

Name_____

goat

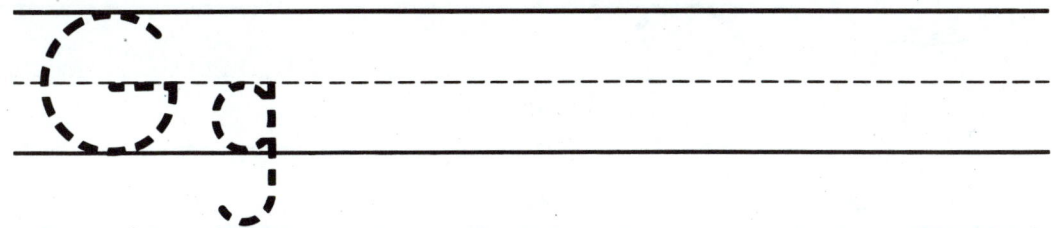

  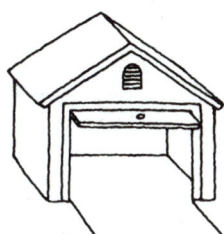 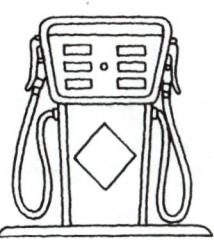

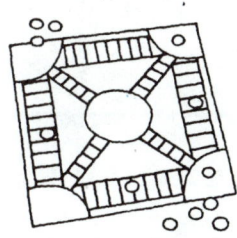   

Directions: Name the pictures. Circle each picture whose name begins with the sound you hear at the beginning of *goat*.

Auditory discrimination of initial *g*

29

Consonants: G

Name _____

goat

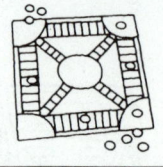      

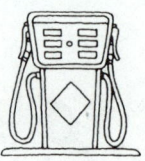      

Directions: Name the pictures. Write the letter *g* below each picture whose name begins with *g*.

30

Sound-symbol association of initial *g*

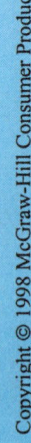

Consonants: *H*

Name_____

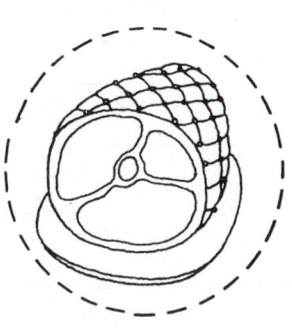
horse

 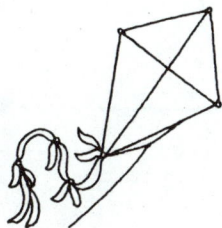 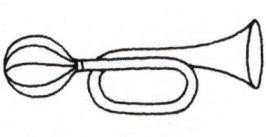 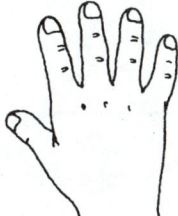

 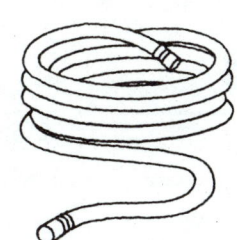  

Directions: Name the pictures. Circle each picture whose name begins with the sound you hear at the beginning of *horse*.

Auditory discrimination of initial *h*

31

Consonants: *H*

Name _____

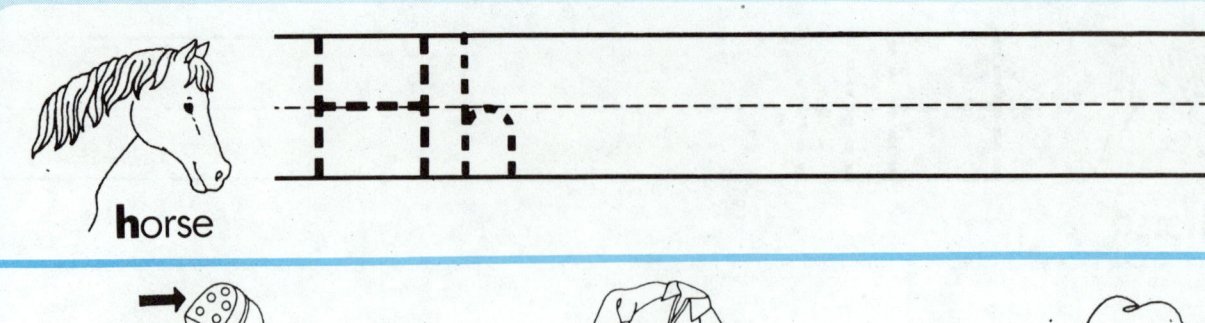
horse

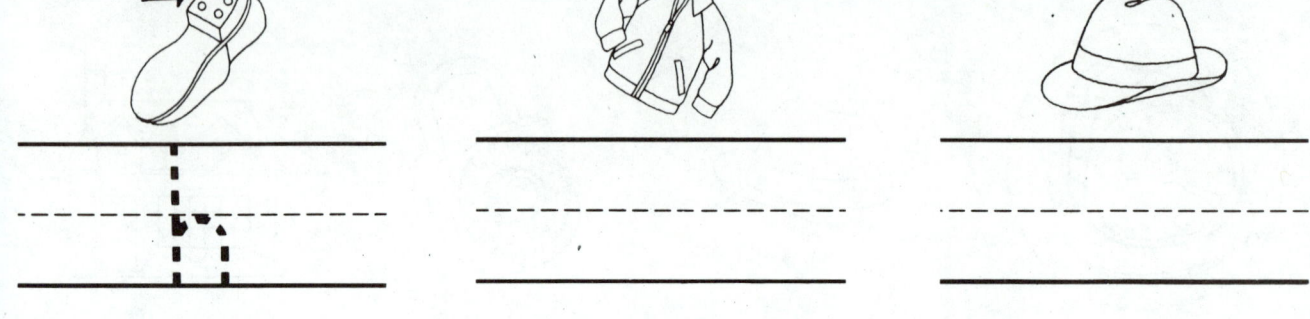

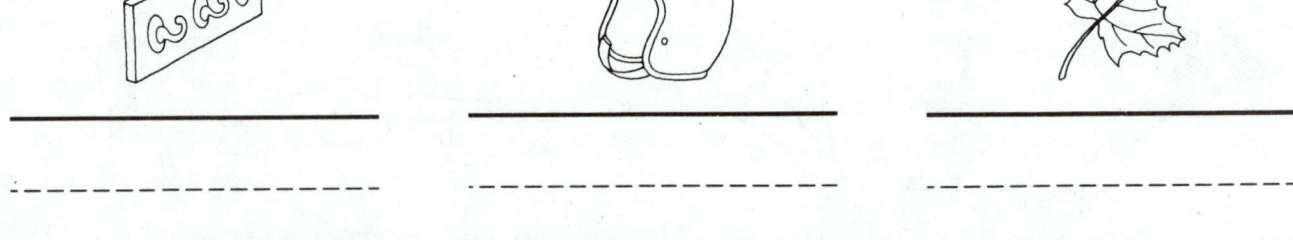

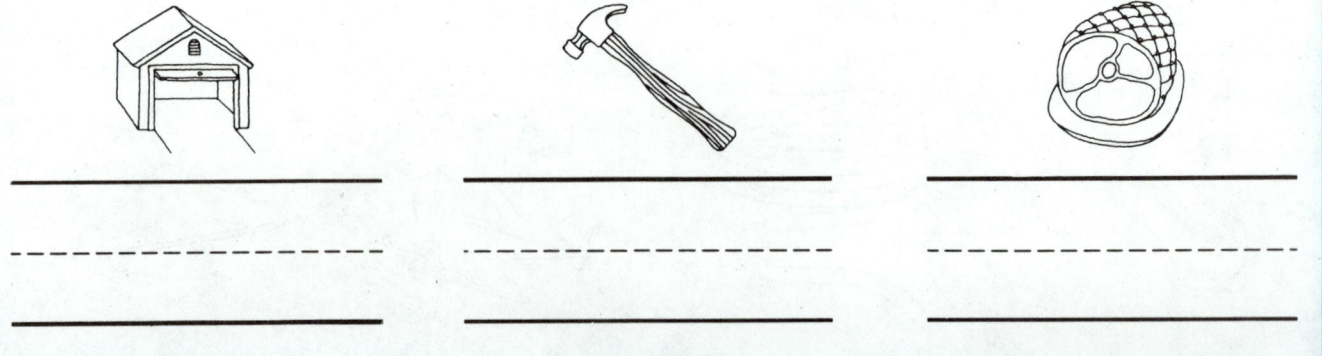

Directions: Name the pictures. Write the letter *h* below each picture whose name begins with *h*.

Sound-symbol association of initial *h*

Matching Letters

Name _____

I i  igloo	J j jet

I	I	H	T	I
i	r	i	t
J	U	J	L	J
j	j	p	j	q

Directions: In each row, circle the letters that are the same as the first letter in the row.

Visual discrimination of capital and lowercase *i* and *j*

33

Matching Letters

Name _____

Ii	igloo		Jj	jet
I	t	i	i	r
i	I	V	H	I
J	i	j	p	j
j	U	J	J	L

Directions: Look at the letter at the beginning of each row. Circle the letters in that row that belong with the first letter.

Matching capital with lowercase *i* and *j*

Short *I*

Name _____

igloo

I i

  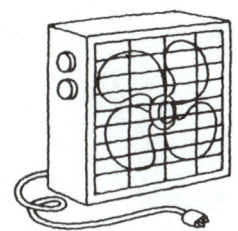 

  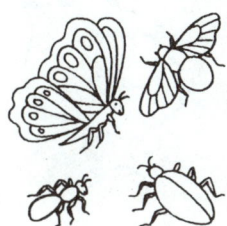 

Directions: Name the pictures. Circle each picture whose name begins with the sound you hear at the beginning of *igloo*.

Auditory discrimination of initial short *i*

Short *I*

Name

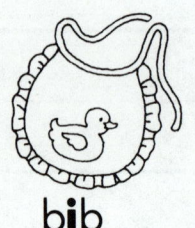
bib

 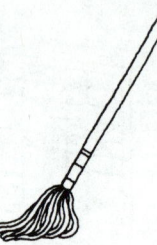  

  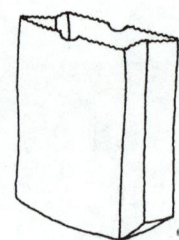 

  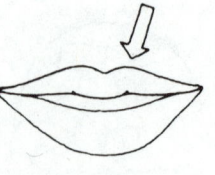 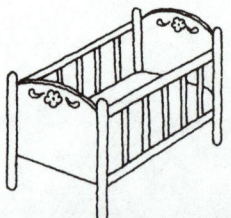

Directions: Name the pictures. Circle each picture whose name has the sound you hear in the middle of *bib*.

36

Auditory discrimination of medial short *i*

Consonants: J

Name _____

jet

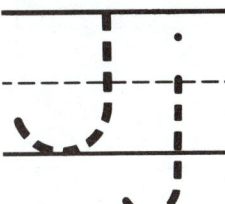

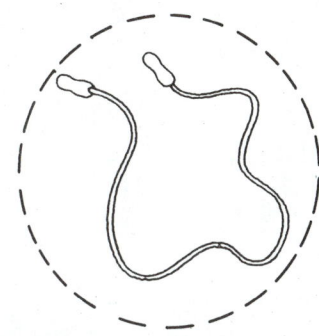

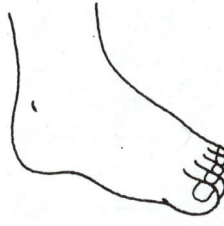

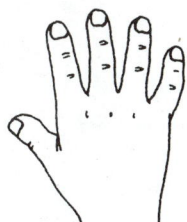

Directions: Name the pictures. Circle each picture whose name begins with the sound you hear at the beginning of *jet*.

Auditory discrimination of initial *j*

Consonants: *J*

Name _____

Directions: Name the pictures. Write the letter *j* below each picture whose name begins with *j*.

38   Sound-symbol association of initial *j*

Matching Letters

Name _____

K k **k**itten	L l **l**ion

K	(K) N R K
k	k l k t
L	J L I L
l	b l l d

Directions: In each row, circle the letters that are the same as the first letter in the row.

Visual discrimination of capital and lowercase *k* and *l*

Matching Letters

Name _____

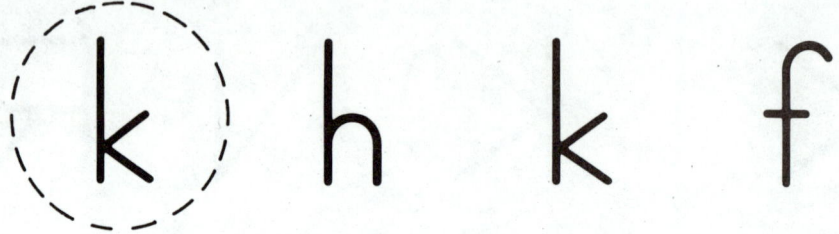

K	k	h	k	f
k	H	K	Y	K
L	l	h	f	l
l	L	T	L	J

Directions: Look at the letter at the beginning of each row. Circle the letters in that row that belong with the first letter.

Consonants: K

Name _____

kitten

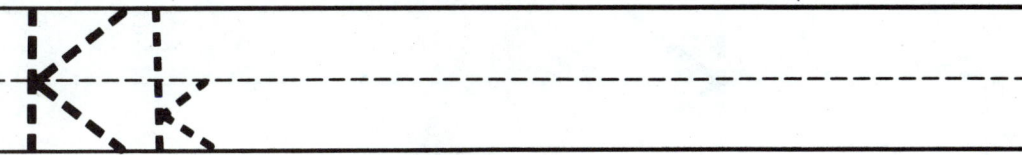

  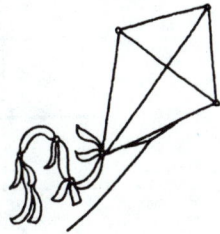 

Directions: Name the pictures. Circle each picture whose name begins with the sound you hear at the beginning of *kitten*.

Auditory discrimination of initial *k*

41

Consonants: *K*

Name _____

 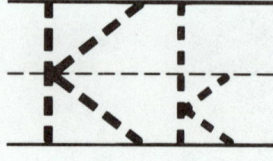

kitten

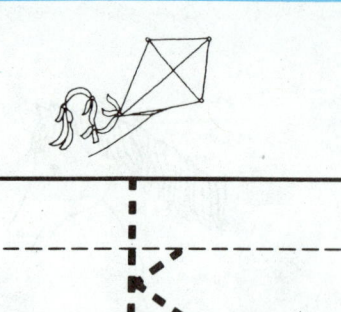  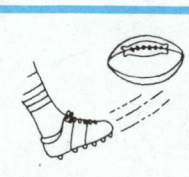

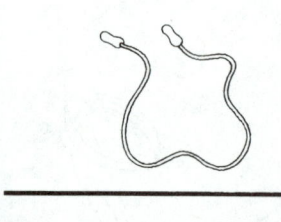  

Directions: Name the pictures. Write the letter *k* below each picture whose name begins with *k*.

Sound-symbol association of initial *k*

REVIEW

G, H, J, K

Name _____

g	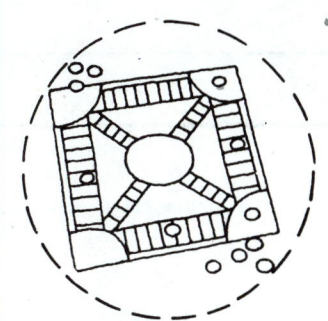		
h		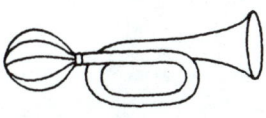	
j			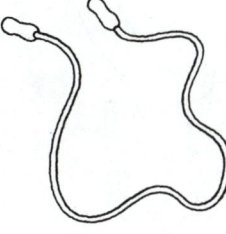
k		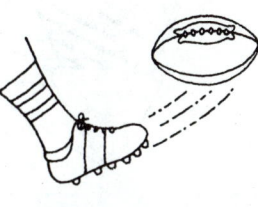	

Directions: Look at the letter at the beginning of each row. Circle each picture in the row whose name begins with the sound made by that letter.

Review of sound-symbol association of initial g, h, j, and k

Consonants: L

Name _____

lion

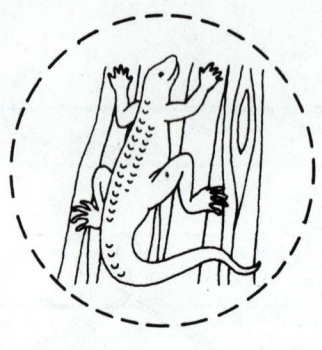 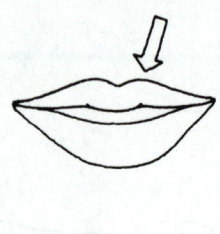  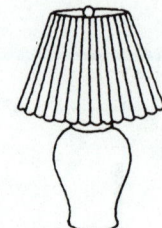

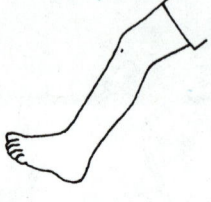   

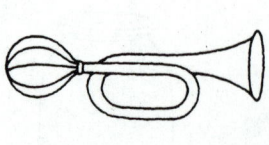   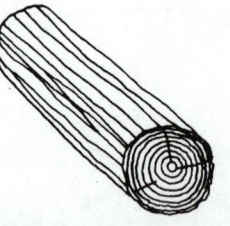

Directions: Name the pictures. Circle each picture whose name begins with the sound you hear at the beginning of *lion.*

44

Auditory discrimination of initial *l*

Consonants: *L*

Name _____

lion

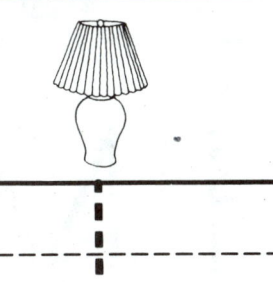  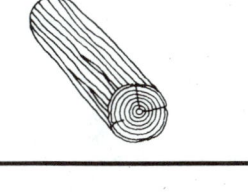

Directions: Name the pictures. Write the letter *l* below each picture whose name begins with *l*.

Sound-symbol association of initial *l*

45

Matching Letters

Name _____

M m **mouse**	N n **nest**
M	W (M) H M
m	m h w m
N	V N N M
n	n m u n

Directions: In each row, circle the letters that are the same as the first letter in the row.

Visual discrimination of capital and lowercase *m* and *n*

Matching Letters

Name _____

M m **m**ouse	N n **n**est
M	n (m) r m
m	M K M N
N	n m n h
n	Y N W N

Directions: Look at the letter at the beginning of each row. Circle the letters in that row that belong with the first letter.

Matching capital with lowercase *m* and *n*

47

Consonants: *M*

Name _____

mouse

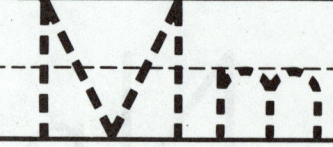

 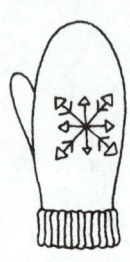  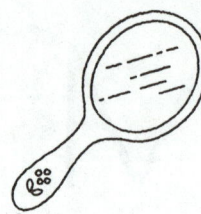

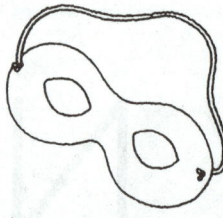 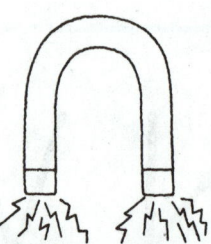  

Directions: Name the pictures. Circle each picture whose name begins with the sound you hear at the beginning of *mouse*.

Auditory discrimination of initial *m*

Consonants: M

Name _____

Mm

mouse

m

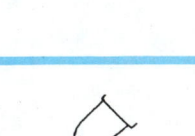 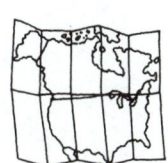 

Directions: Name the pictures. Write the letter *m* below each picture whose name begins with *m*.

Sound-symbol association of initial *m*

49

Consonants: N

Name _____

nest

Nn

   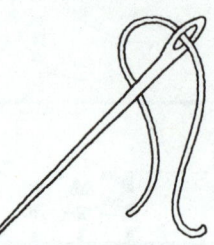

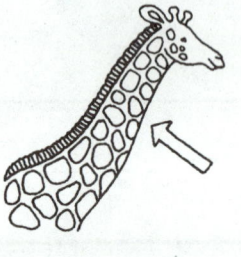 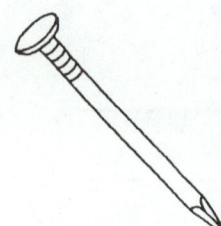  

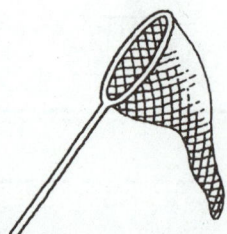   

Directions: Name the pictures. Circle each picture whose name begins with the sound you hear at the beginning of *nest*.

50

Auditory discrimination of initial *n*

Consonants: N

Name _____

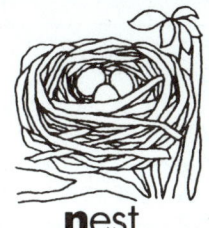

nest

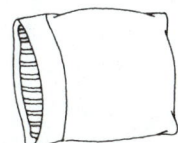

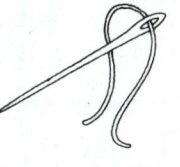

Directions: Name the pictures. Write the letter *n* below each picture whose name begins with *n*.

Matching Letters

Name _____

O o *octopus*				P p *pig*	
O	O	Q	C	O	
o	c	o	u	o	
P	B	P	P	R	
p	p	q	p	j	

Directions: In each row, circle the letters that are the same as the first letter in the row.

Visual discrimination of capital and lowercase *o* and *p*

Matching Letters

Name _____

O o	 octopus	P p	pig
O	o	p	o	c
o	Q	O	U	O
P	p	y	o	p
p	D	P	P	B

Directions: Look at the letter at the beginning of each row. Circle the letters in that row that belong with the first letter.

Matching capital with lowercase *o* and *p*

53

Short O

Name _____

octopus

  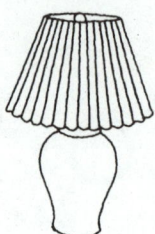 

 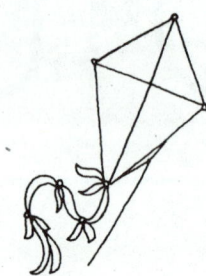  

  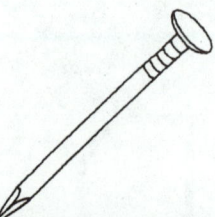 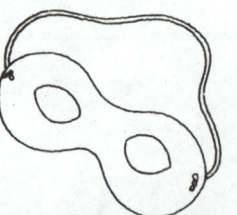

Directions: Name the pictures. Circle each picture whose name begins with the sound you hear at the beginning of *octopus*.

Auditory discrimination of initial short *o*

Short o

Name _____

top

 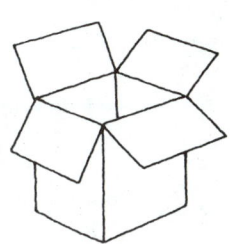  

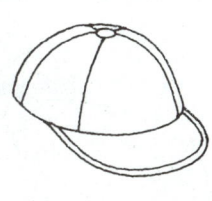  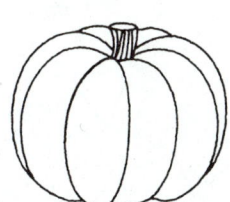 

Directions: Name the pictures. Circle each picture whose name has the sound you hear in the middle of *top*.

Auditory discrimination of medial short *o*

I and *O*

Name _____

Directions: Look at the picture at the beginning of each row. Circle each picture in the row whose name begins with the same sound as the first picture.

Directions: Look at the picture at the beginning of each row. Circle each picture in the row whose name has the same middle sound as the first picture.

Review of auditory discrimination of short *i* and short *o* in initial and medial positions

Consonants: P

Name _____

pig

B b

 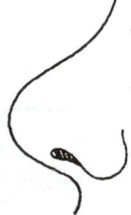 

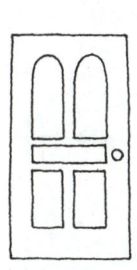   

Directions: Name the pictures. Circle each picture whose name begins with the sound you hear at the beginning of *pig*.

Auditory discrimination of initial *p*

57

Consonants: P

Name _____

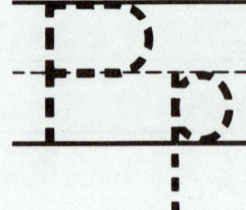

pig

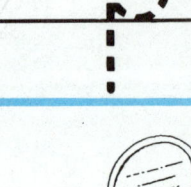 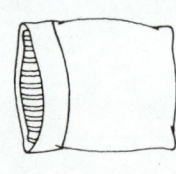 

 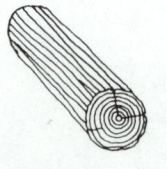 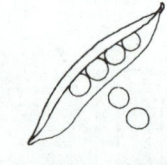

Directions: Name the pictures. Write the letter *p* below each picture whose name begins with *p*.

58

Sound-symbol association of initial *p*

REVIEW

L, M, N, P

Name _____

l		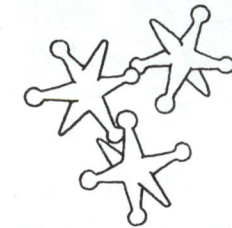	
m	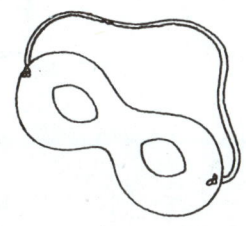		
n	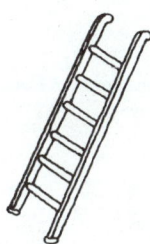		
p			

Directions: Look at the letter at the beginning of each row. Circle each picture in the row whose name begins with the sound made by that letter.

Review of sound-symbol association of initial *l, m, n,* and *p*

Matching Letters

Name _____

Q q *quilt*	R r *rose*

Q	Q	O	D	Q
q	q	j	q	p
R	P	R	B	R
r	h	r	r	m

Directions: In each row, circle the letters that are the same as the first letter in the row.

60

Visual discrimination of capital and lowercase *q* and *r*

Matching Letters

Name _____

Q q	quilt	R r	rose

Q	e	(q)	q	d

q	Q	O	U	Q

R	r	n	m	r

r	P	R	B	R

Directions: Look at the letter at the beginning of each row. Circle the letters in that row that belong with the first letter.

Matching capital with lowercase *q* and *r*

Consonants: *Qu*

Name _____

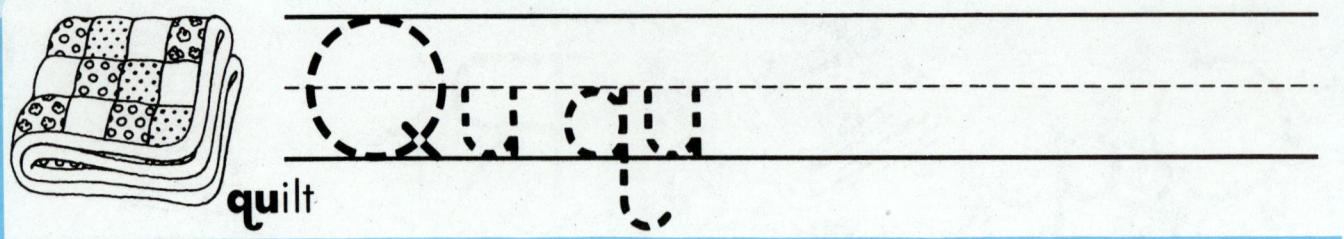
quilt

  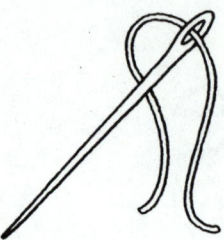 

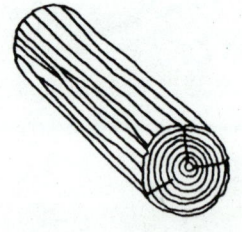   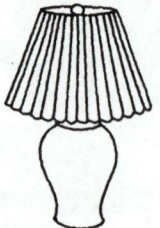

 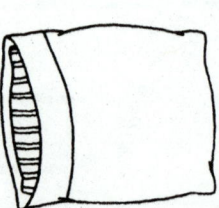  

Directions: Name the pictures. Circle each picture whose name begins with the sound you hear at the beginning of *quilt*.

62

Auditory discrimination of initial *qu*

Consonants: *Qu*

Name _____

quilt

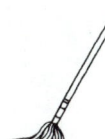

Directions: Name the pictures. Write the letters *qu* below each picture whose name begins with *qu*.

Sound-symbol association of initial *qu*

63

Consonants: R

Name _____

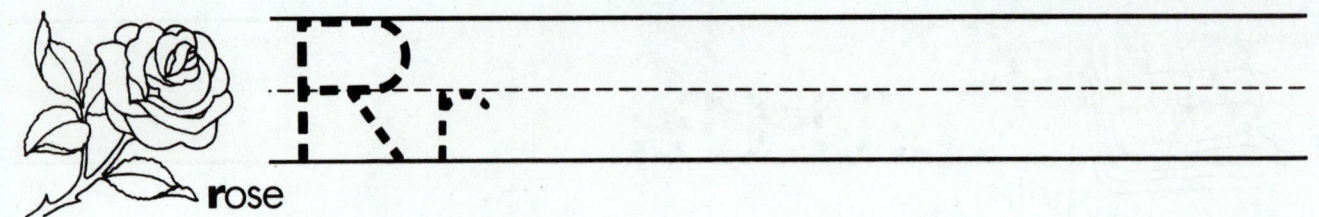
rose

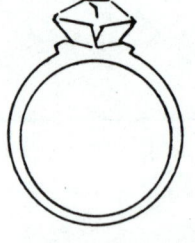   

 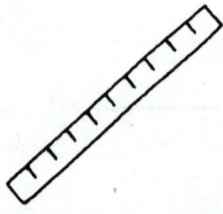 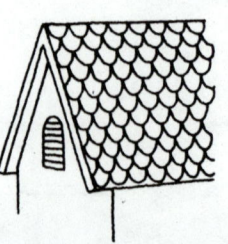 

Directions: Name the pictures. Circle each picture whose name begins with the sound you hear at the beginning of *rose*.

Auditory discrimination of initial r

Consonants: R

Name_____

R r

rose

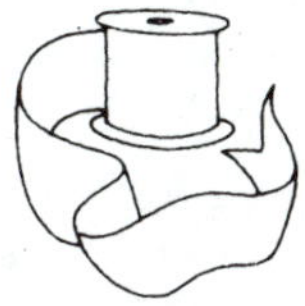

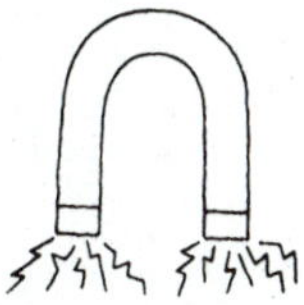

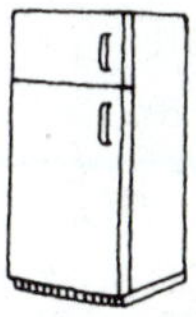

Directions: Name the pictures. Write the letter *r* below each picture whose name begins with *r*.

Sound-symbol association of initial *r*

65

Matching Letters

Name _____

Ss ☀ sun	Tt ⛺ tent
S	S Z G S
s	z s e s
T	T L T Y
t	h t t l

Directions: In each row, circle the letters that are the same as the first letter in the row.

Visual discrimination of capital and lowercase *s* and *t*

Matching Letters

Name_____

Ss	 sun	**Tt**	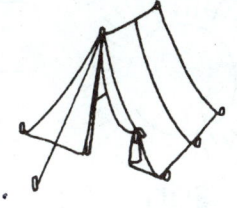 tent	
S		c	s	o
s	G	S	C	S
T	l	t	t	i
t	T	Y	T	X

Directions: Look at the letter at the beginning of each row. Circle the letters in that row that belong with the first letter.

Matching capital with lowercase *s* and *t*

67

Consonants: S

Name _____

sun

Ss

 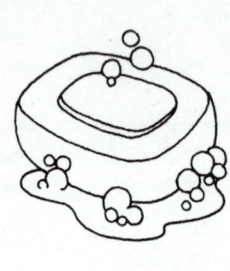 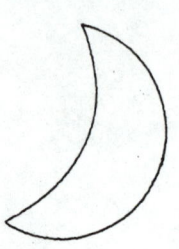 

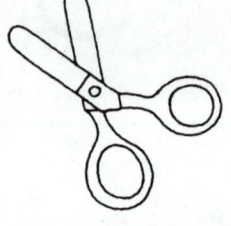 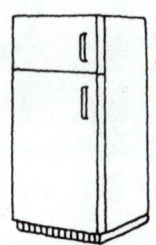  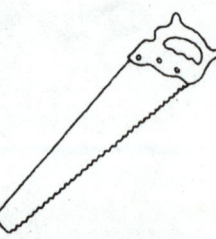

  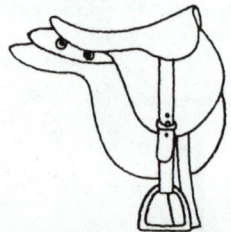 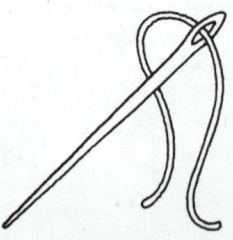

Directions: Name the pictures. Circle each picture whose name begins with the sound you hear at the beginning of *sun*.

68
Auditory discrimination of initial *s*

Consonants: *S*

Name _____

sun

Ss

---

s

Directions: Name the pictures. Write the letter *s* below each picture whose name begins with *s*.

Sound-symbol association of initial *s*

69

Consonants: *T*

Name_____

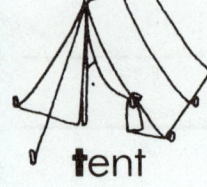
tent

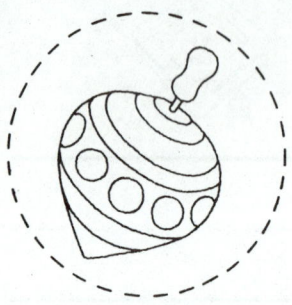   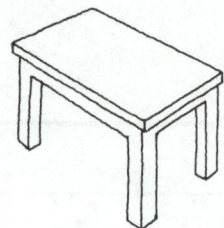

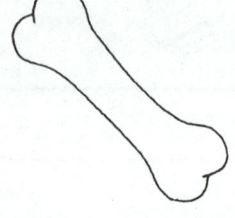 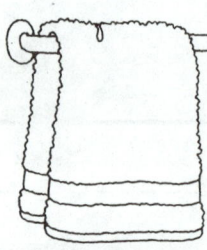  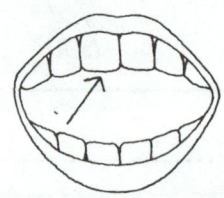

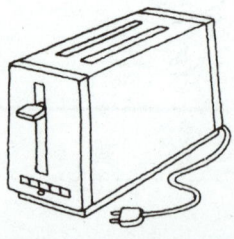 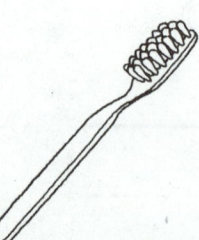 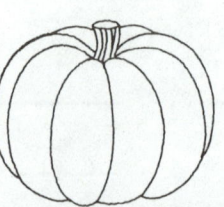 

Directions: Name the pictures. Circle each picture whose name begins with the sound you hear at the beginning of *tent*.

Auditory discrimination of initial *t*

Consonants: *T*

Name _____

tent

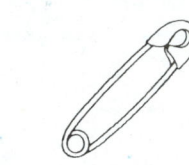

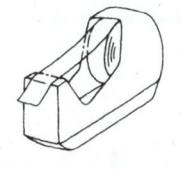

Directions: Name the pictures. Write the letter *t* below each picture whose name begins with *t*.

Sound-symbol association of initial *t*

71

REVIEW

Qu, R, S, T

Name _____

qu			
r		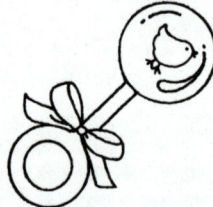	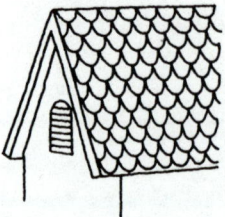
s			
t			

Directions: Look at the letter or letters at the beginning of each row. Circle each picture in the row whose name begins with the sound made by that letter.

Review of sound-symbol association of initial *qu, r, s,* and *t*

Matching Letters

Name _____

U u	 **u**mbrella	V v	 **v**ase
U	O		J U
u	u	n	c u
V	X	V	V N
v	v	u	z v

Directions: In each row, circle the letters that are the same as the first letter in the row.

Visual discrimination of capital and lowercase *u* and *v*

Matching Letters

Name _____

U u	 **u**mbrella	V v	 **v**ase

U	v	(u)	n	u

u	U	O	U	C

V	w	v	u	v

v	V	N	Y	V

Directions: Look at the letter at the beginning of each row. Circle the letters in that row that belong with the first letter.

Matching capital with lowercase *u* and *v*

Short *U*

Name _____

umbrella

  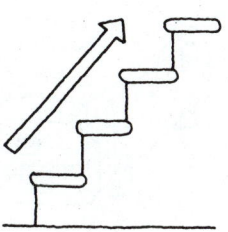 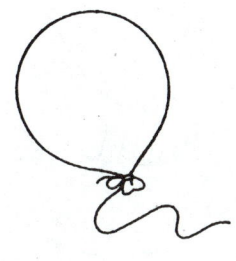

 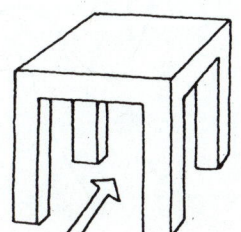 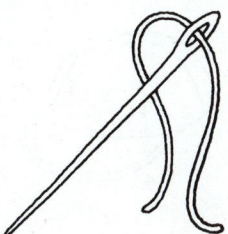 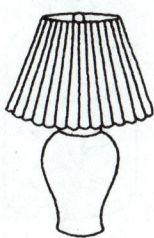

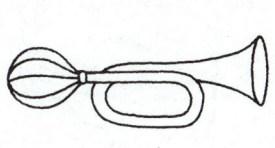   

Directions: Name the pictures. Circle each picture whose name begins with the sound you hear at the beginning of *umbrella*.

Auditory discrimination of initial short *u*

Short *U*

Name _____

cup

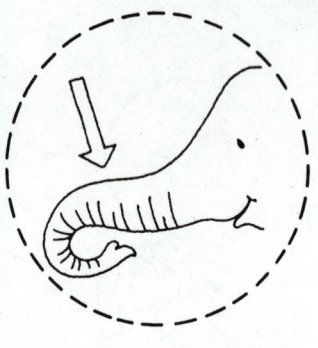   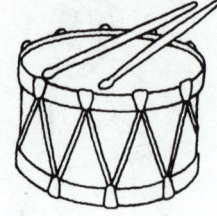

 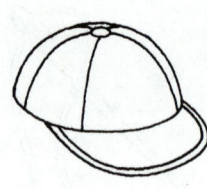  

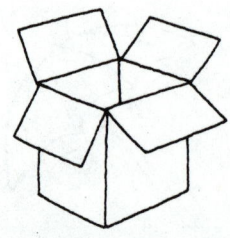   

Directions: Name the pictures. Circle each picture whose name has the sound you hear in the middle of *cup*.

Auditory discrimination of medial short *u*

REVIEW: Short *U*

Name _____

Directions: Look at the picture at the beginning of each row. Circle each picture in the row whose name begins with the same sound as the first picture.

 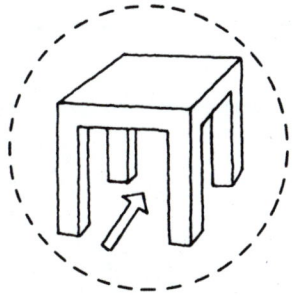  

  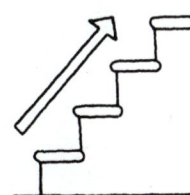 

Directions: Look at the picture at the beginning of each row. Circle each picture in the row whose name has the same middle sound as the first picture.

 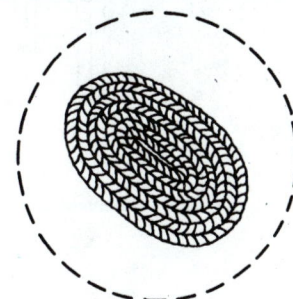 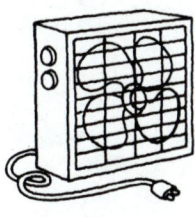 

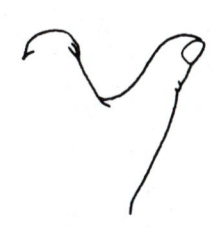   

Review of auditory discrimination of short *u* in initial and medial positions

Consonants: *V*

Name _____

 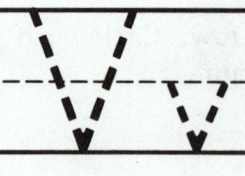
vase

  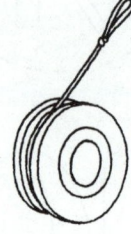 

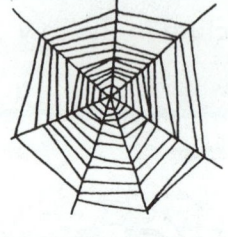  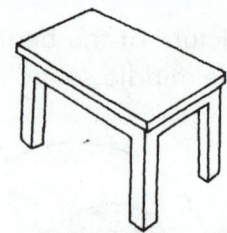 

Directions: Name the pictures. Circle each picture whose name begins with the sound you hear at the beginning of *vase*.

78

Auditory discrimination of initial *v*

Consonants: v

Name_____

vase

Directions: Name the pictures. Write the letter v below each picture whose name begins with v.

Sound-symbol association of initial v

79

Matching Letters

Name _____

| W w | watch | X x | ax |

W	N	(W)	Y	W
w	w	v	x	w
X	Z	X	X	Y
x	x	y	x	t

Directions: In each row, circle the letters that are the same as the first letter in the row.

80   Visual discrimination of capital and lowercase *w* and *x*

Matching Letters

Name _____

W w	X x
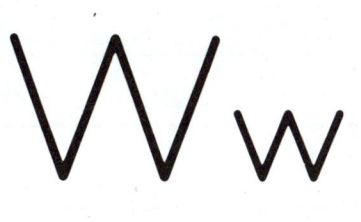 **w**atch	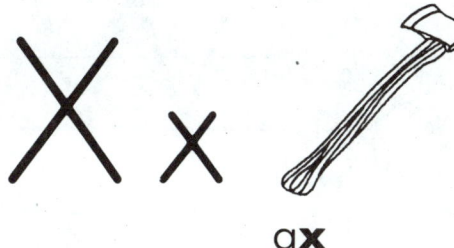 a**x**

W	v w m w
w	W K W Z
X	x t v x
x	Y X Z X

Directions: Look at the letter at the beginning of each row. Circle the letters in that row that belong with the first letter.

Matching capital with lowercase *w* and *x*

Consonants: W

Name_____

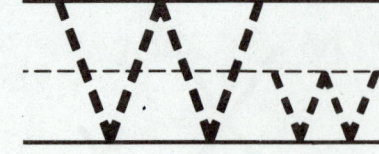

watch

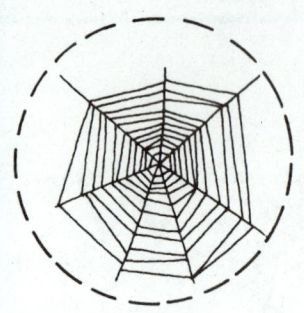 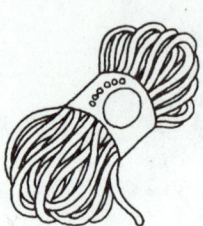  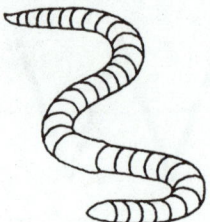

 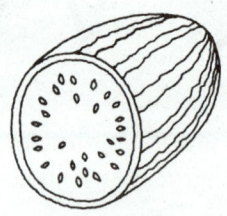  

Directions: Name the pictures. Circle each picture whose name begins with the sound you hear at the beginning of *watch*.

Auditory discrimination of initial *w*

Consonants: W

Name _____

W w

watch

Directions: Name the pictures. Write the letter *w* below each picture whose name begins with *w*.

Sound-symbol association of initial *w*

83

Consonants: X

Name_____

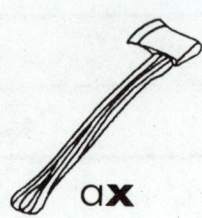 a**x**

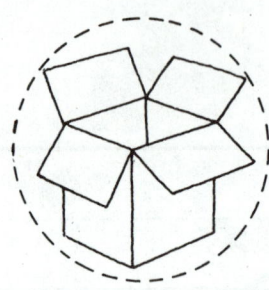   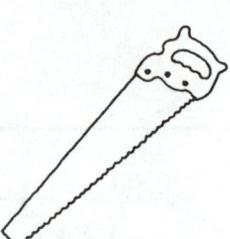

  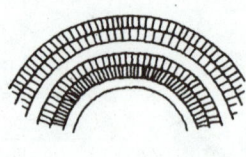 

 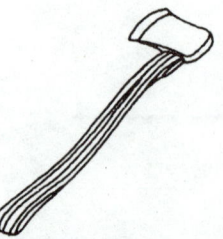  

Directions: Name the pictures. Circle each picture whose name ends with the sound you hear at the end of *ax*.

Auditory discrimination of final *x*

Consonants: X

Name _____

 ax

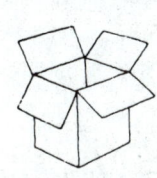

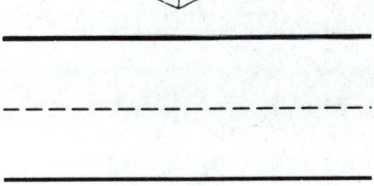

Directions: Name the pictures. Write the letter *x* below each picture whose name ends with *x*.

Sound-symbol association of final *x*

85

Matching Letters

Name _____

| Y y | 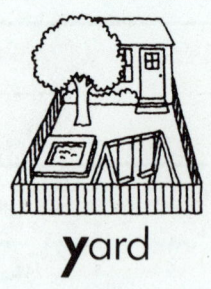 **y**ard | Z z |  **z**oo |

Y	Y	T	K	Y
y	v	y	w	y
Z	Z	N	Z	I
z	z	s	w	z

Directions: In each row, circle the letters that are the same as the first letter in the row.

86

Visual discrimination of capital and lowercase *y* and *z*

Matching Letters

Name _____

Y	 yard		Z z	 zoo
Y	x	 y (circled)	h	y
y	Y	T	Y	K
Z	s	z	z	c
z	N	Z	I	Z

Directions: Look at the letter at the beginning of each row. Circle the letters in that row that belong with the first letter.

Matching capital with lowercase *y* and *z*

87

Consonants: Y

Name _____

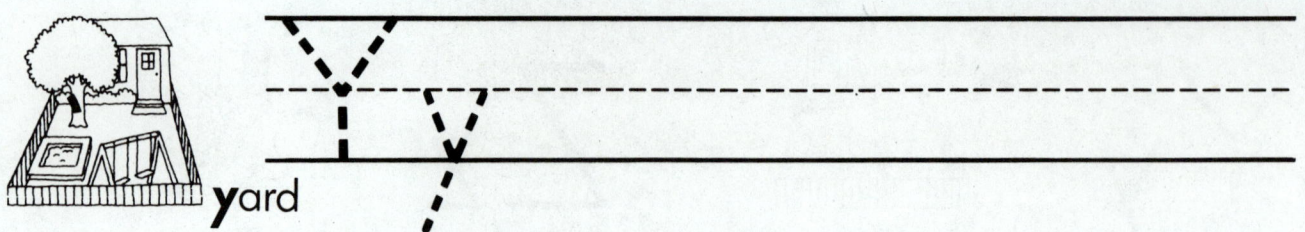
yard

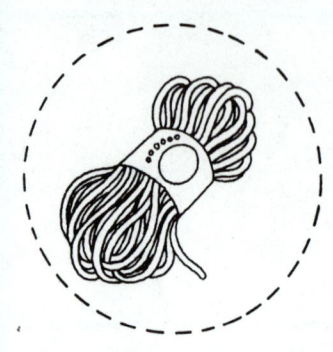 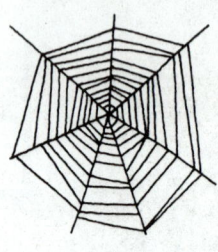 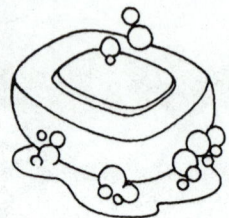 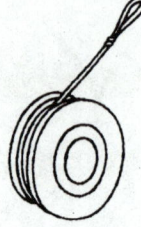

 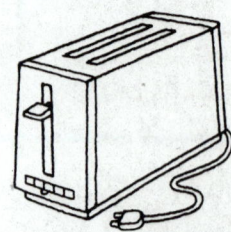  

Directions: Name the pictures. Circle each picture whose name begins with the sound you hear at the beginning of *yard*.

88

Auditory discrimination of initial *y*

Consonants: Y

Name _____

Y Y

yard

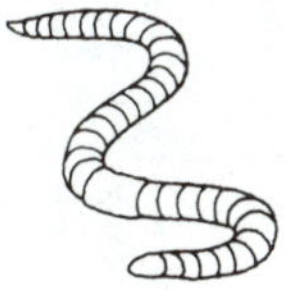

Directions: Name the pictures. Write the letter *y* below each picture whose name begins with *y*.

Sound-symbol association of initial *y*

89

Consonants: Z

Name _____

zoo

 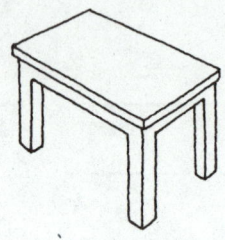  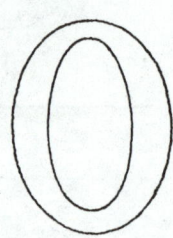

 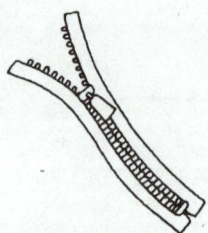  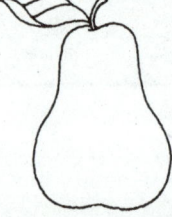

   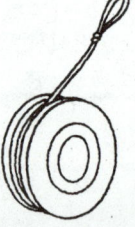

Directions: Name the pictures. Circle each picture whose name begins with the sound you hear at the beginning of *zoo*.

Auditory discrimination of initial z

Consonants: Z

Name

zoo

Directions: Name the pictures. Write the letter *z* below each picture whose name begins with *z*.

Sound-symbol association of initial *z*

91

REVIEW

V, W, X, Y, Z

Name _____

v	vest	web	van
w	well	wagon	(giraffe/kangaroo)
x	(boy — ax)	ax	fox
y	yo-yo	yarn	vase
z	zebra	(valentine)	zipper

Directions: Look at the letter at the beginning of each row. Circle each picture in the row whose name has the sound made by that letter.

Review of sound-symbol association of initial *v*, *w*, final *x*, initial *y*, and *z*.

Consonants

Name _____

(r) f v 	b k x 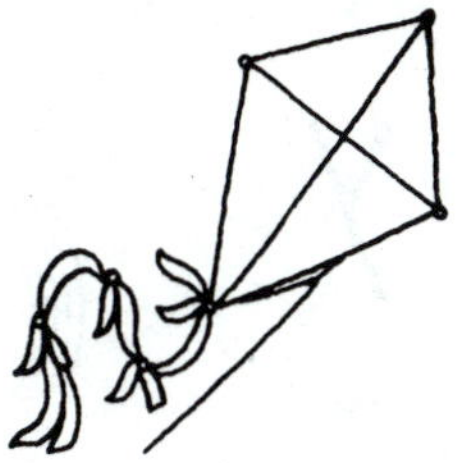	b c t 
h j n 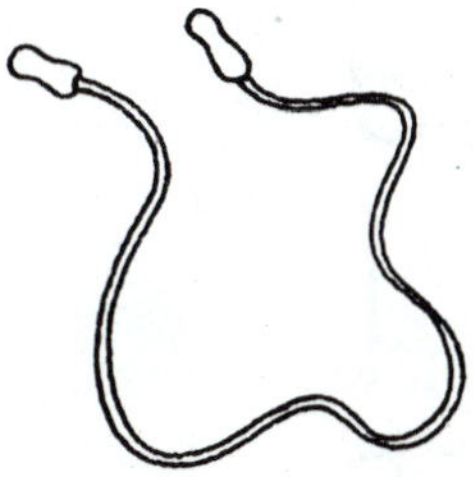	g j z 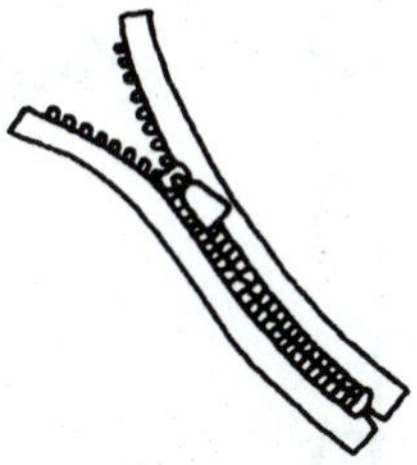	r d t 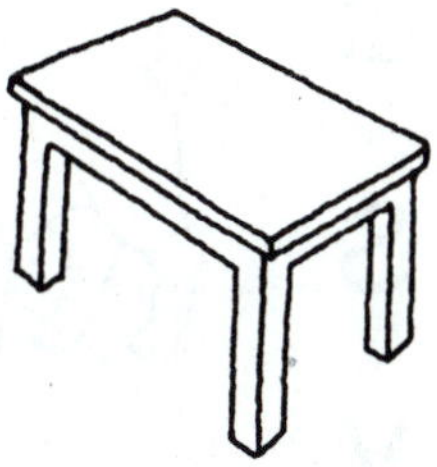
m p v 	n s w 	j m n 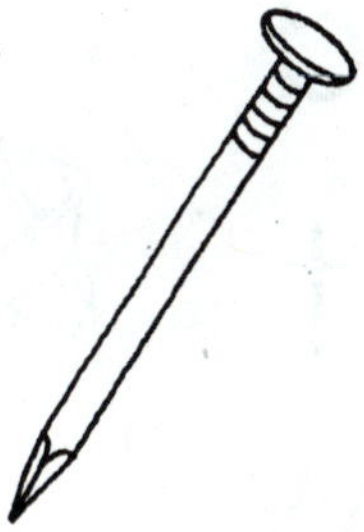
d f g 	qu r y 	l v z 

Directions: Name the pictures. Circle the letter that stands for the sound at the beginning of each picture name.

Assessment of sound-symbol association of initial consonants

Consonants

Name _____

k (p) v	t y z	c d f
d s v	b n h	j l s
d t w	c g l	f r z
l n y	b k w	x j m

Directions: Name the pictures. Circle the letter that stands for the sound at the beginning of each picture name.

Vowels

Name _____

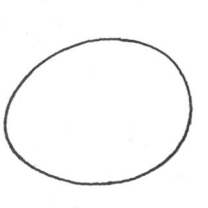  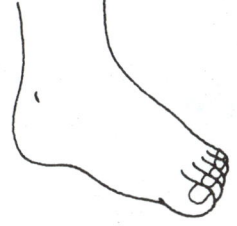 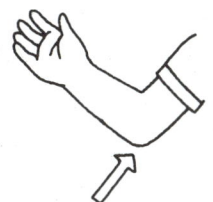
 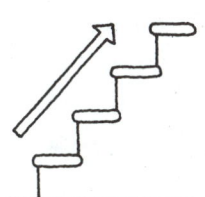  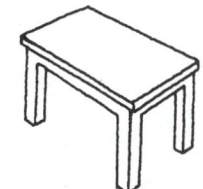

Directions: Name the first picture in each row. Then circle all the pictures in that row that begin with the same sound as the first picture.

Assessment of auditory discrimination of initial vowels

95

Sounds and Letters

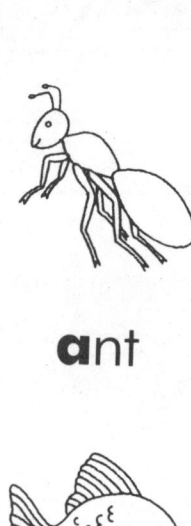    

ant **b**all **c**ar **d**og **e**lephant

fish **g**oat **h**orse **i**gloo **j**et

   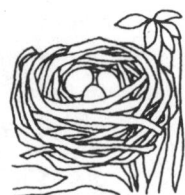 

kitten **l**ion **m**ouse **n**est **o**ctopus

    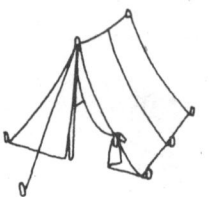

pig **qu**ilt **r**ose **s**un **t**ent

umbrella **v**ase **w**atch a**x** **y**ard **z**oo

Completing Pictures

Name _____

Directions: Complete each picture by tracing the dotted lines. Color each picture.

Eye-hand coordination

3

Moving from Left to Right

Name _____

Directions: Beginning at the black dot, trace the dotted line in each picture, moving from left to right.

4

Left-to-right progression

Matching Pictures

Name _____

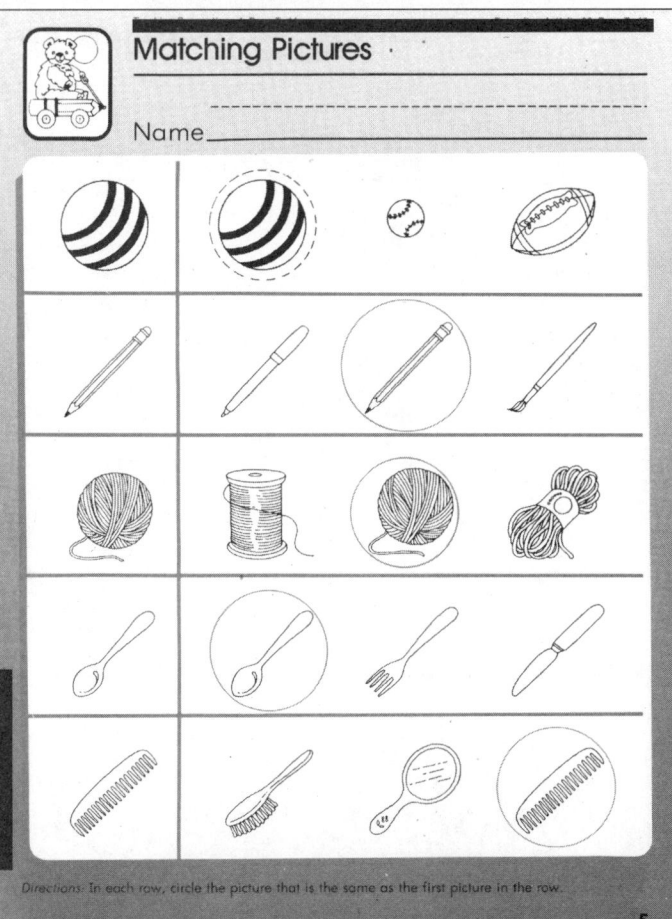

Directions: In each row, circle the picture that is the same as the first picture in the row.

Visual discrimination of pictures

5

Matching Pictures

Name _____

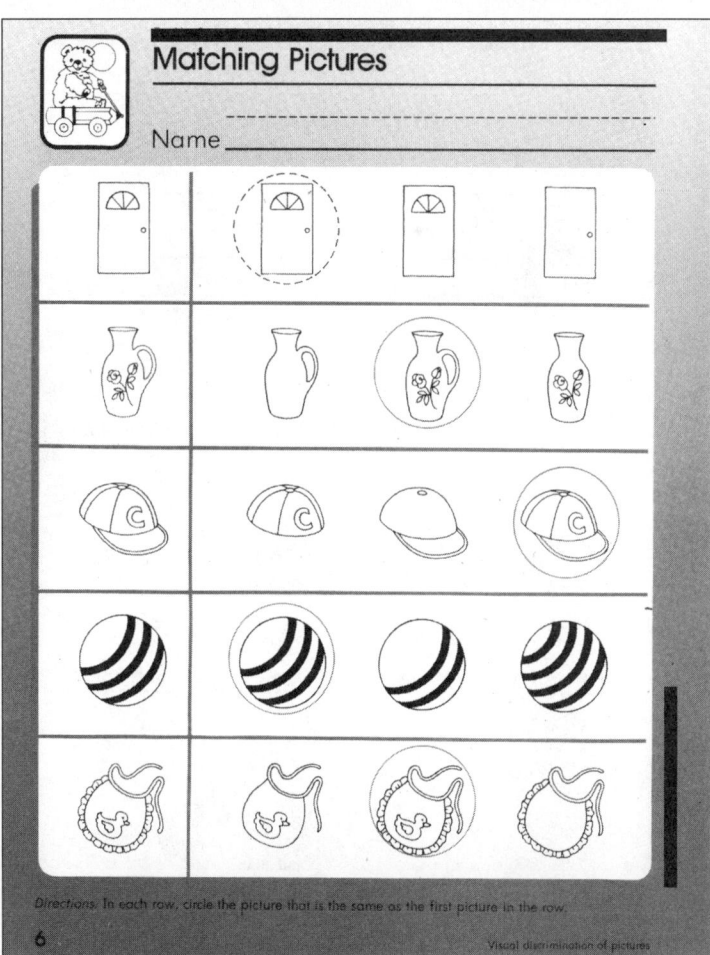

Directions: In each row, circle the picture that is the same as the first picture in the row.

6

Visual discrimination of pictures

97

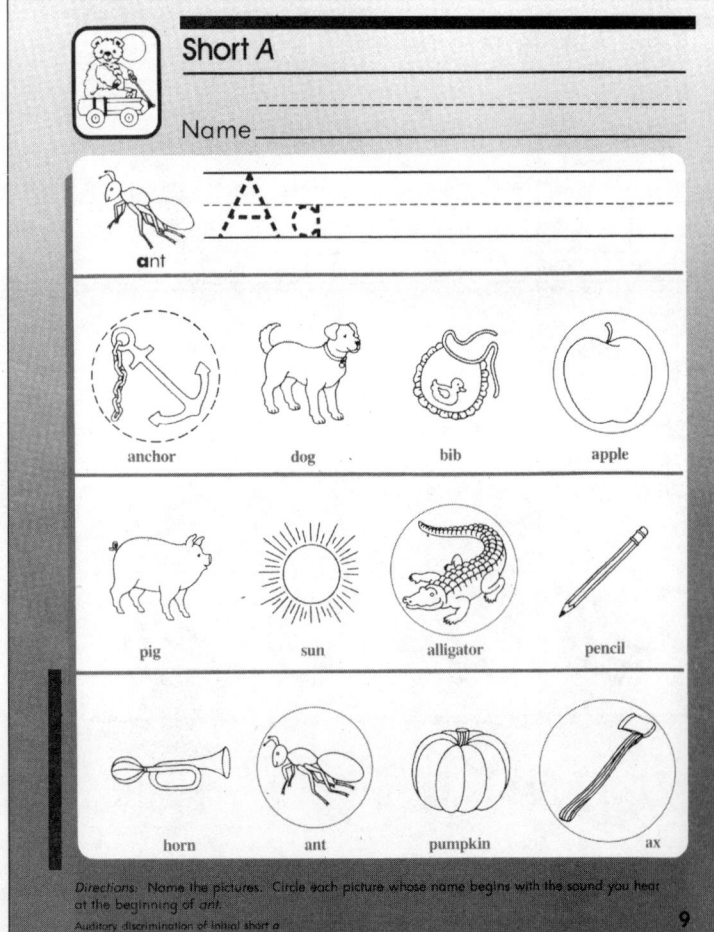
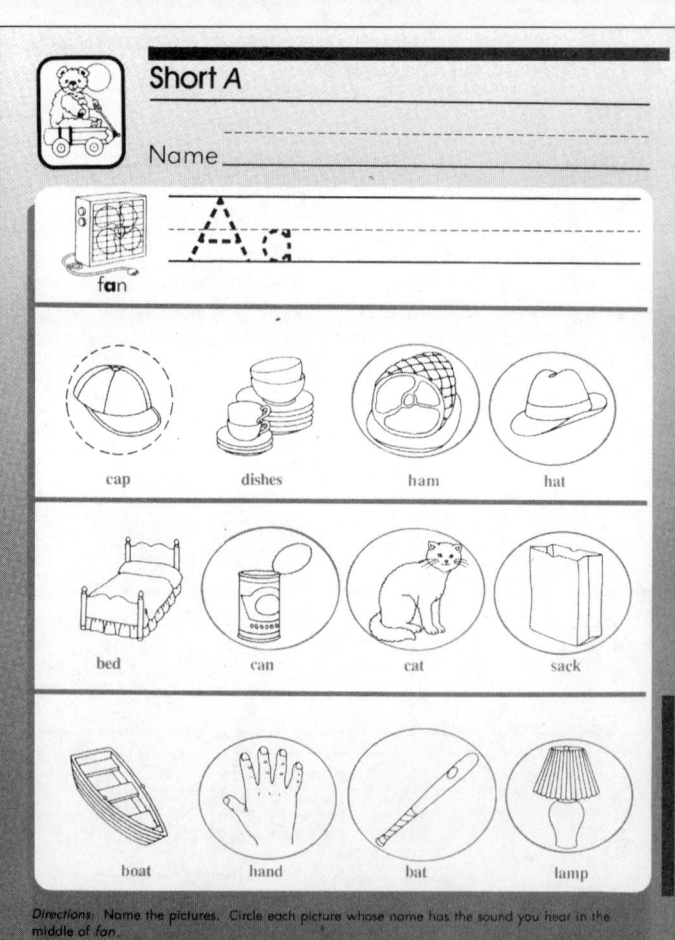

Consonants: B

Name _____

Directions: Name the pictures. Circle each picture whose name begins with the sound you hear at the beginning of ball.

Auditory discrimination of initial b

Consonants: B

Name _____

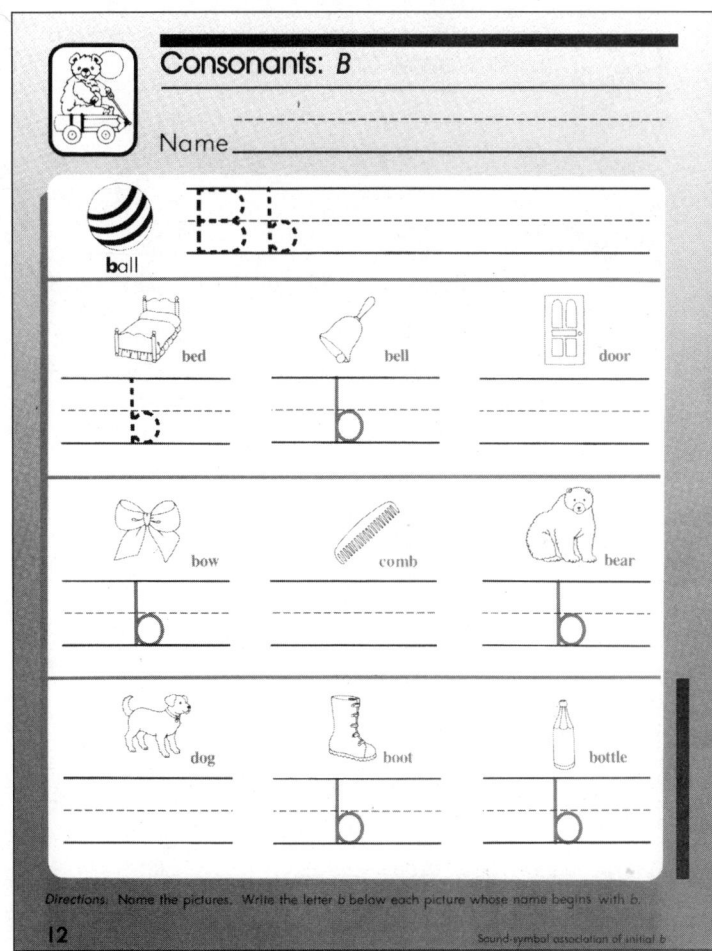

Directions: Name the pictures. Write the letter b below each picture whose name begins with b.

Sound-symbol association of initial b

Matching Letters

Name _____

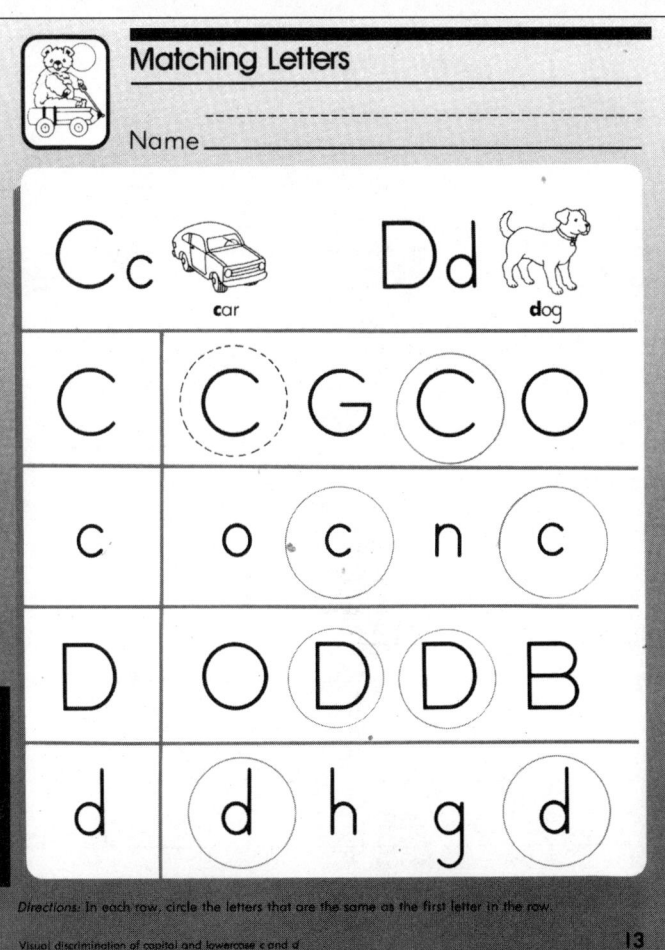

Directions: In each row, circle the letters that are the same as the first letter in the row.

Visual discrimination of capital and lowercase c and d

Matching Letters

Name _____

Directions: Look at the letter at the beginning of each row. Circle the letters in that row that belong with the first letter.

Matching capital with lowercase c and d

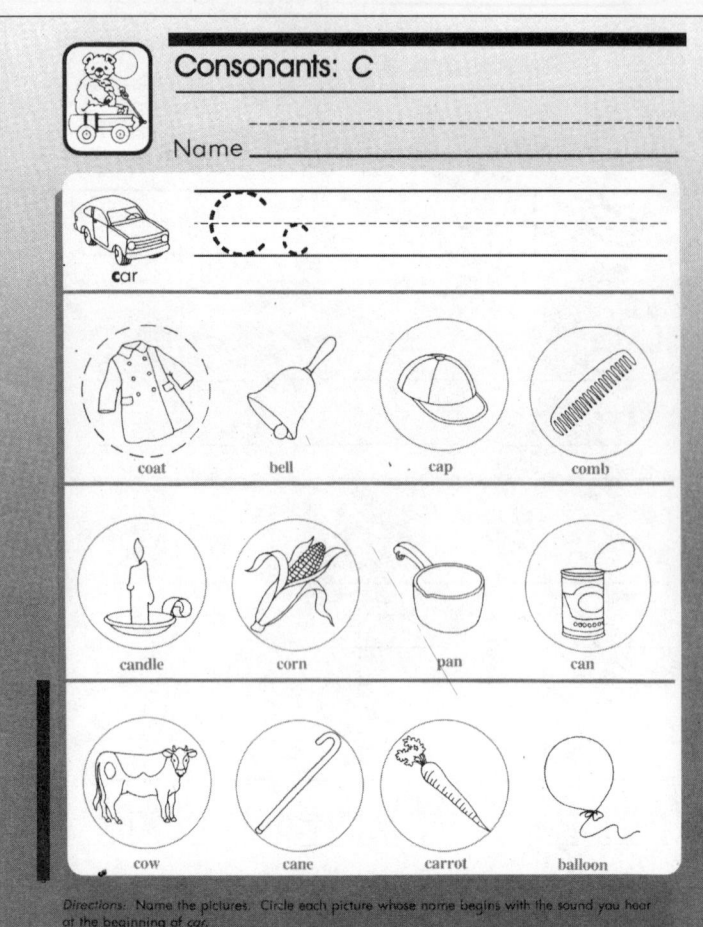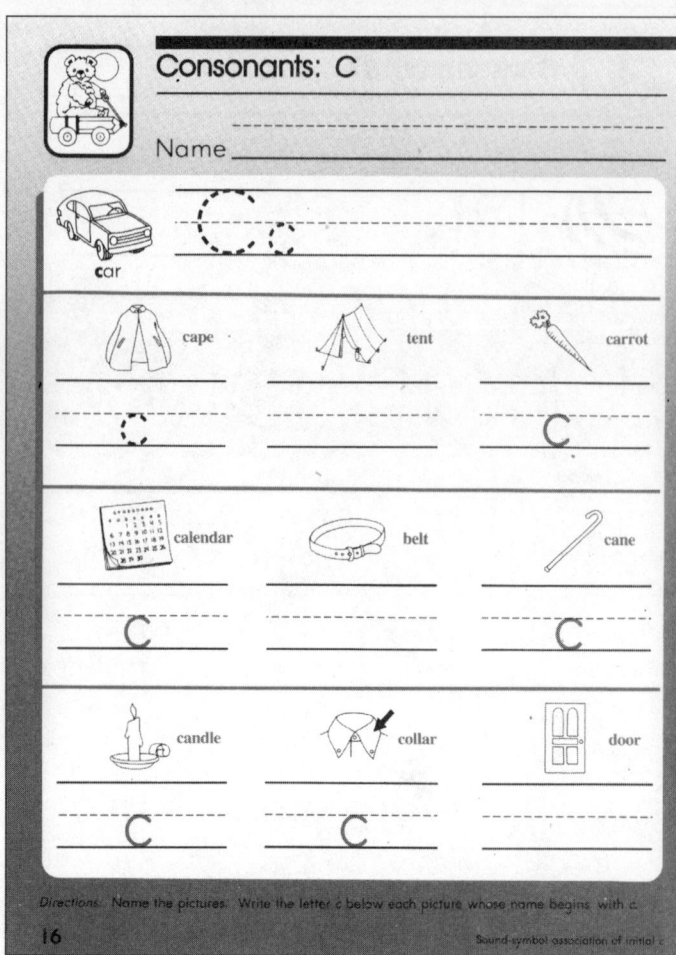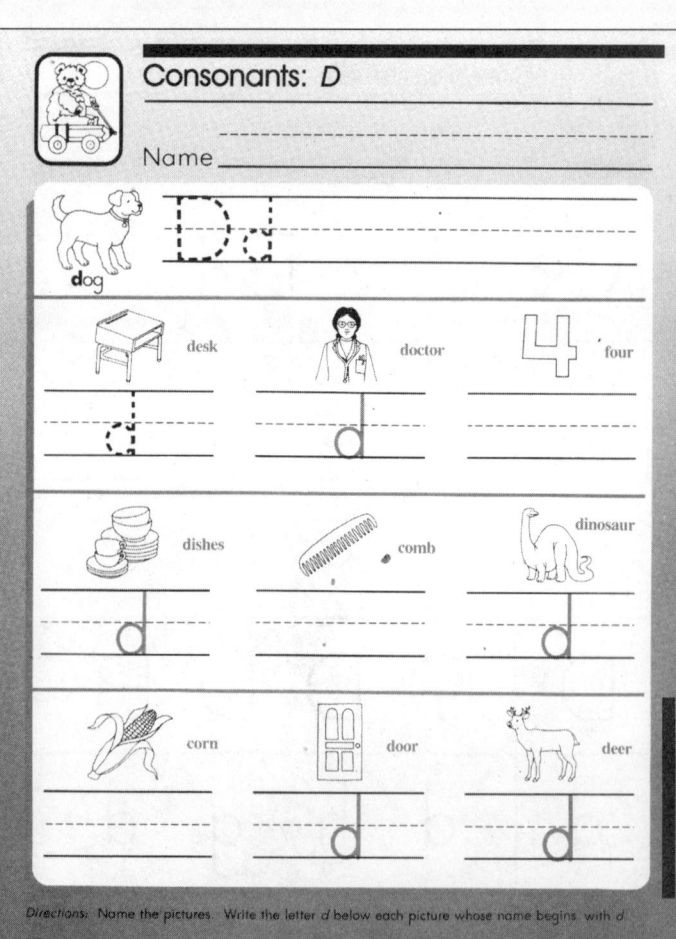

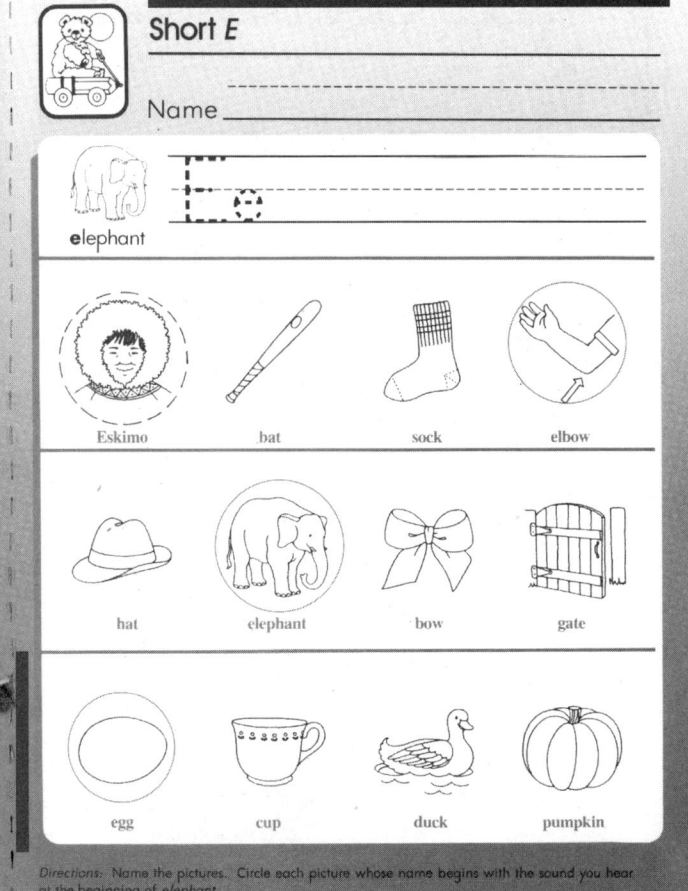

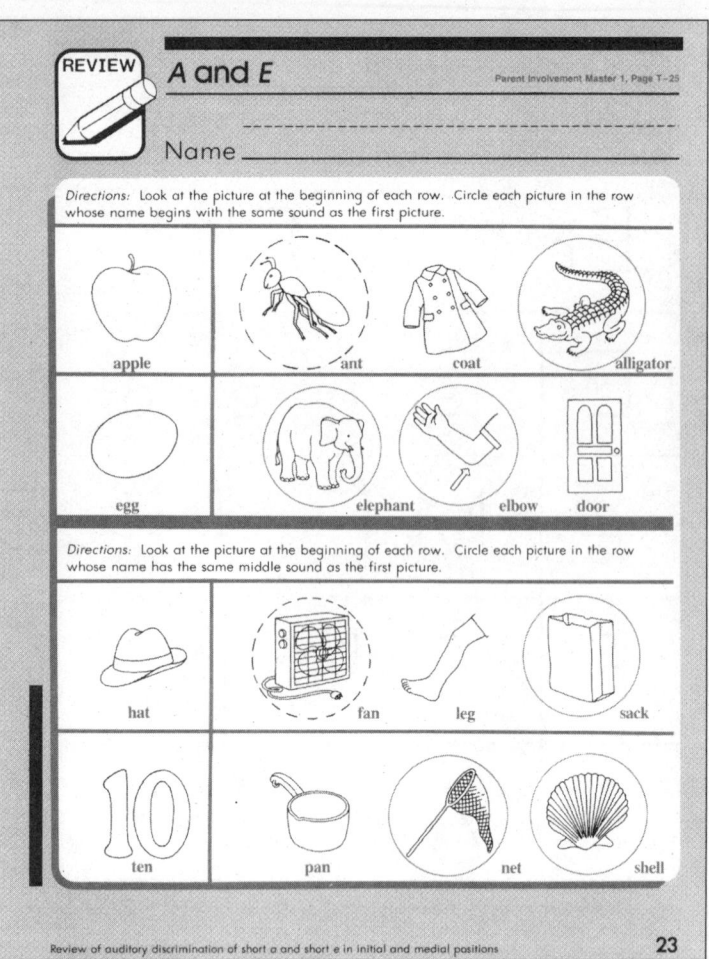
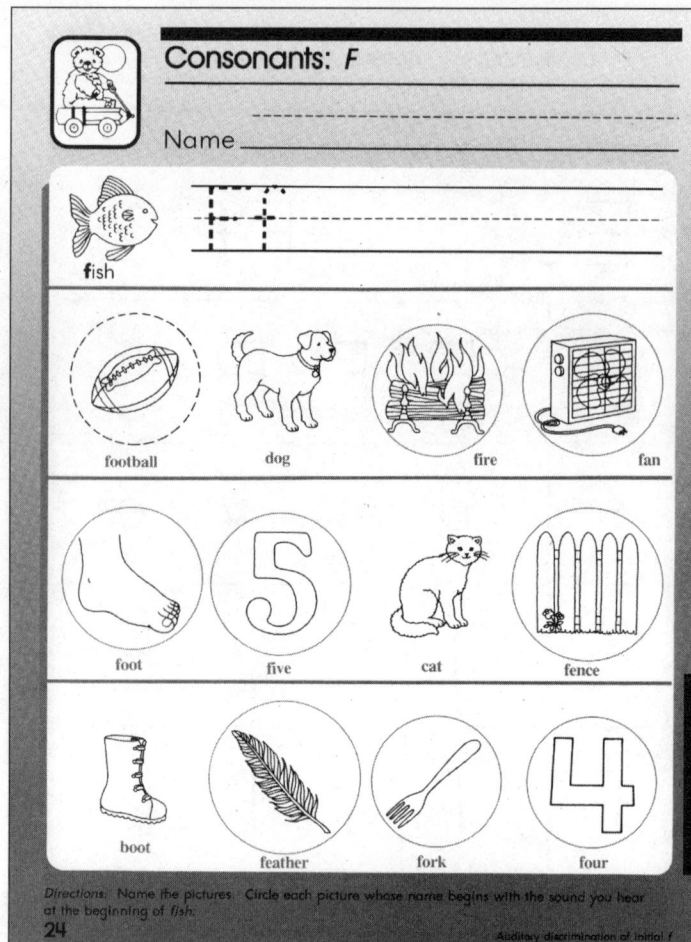
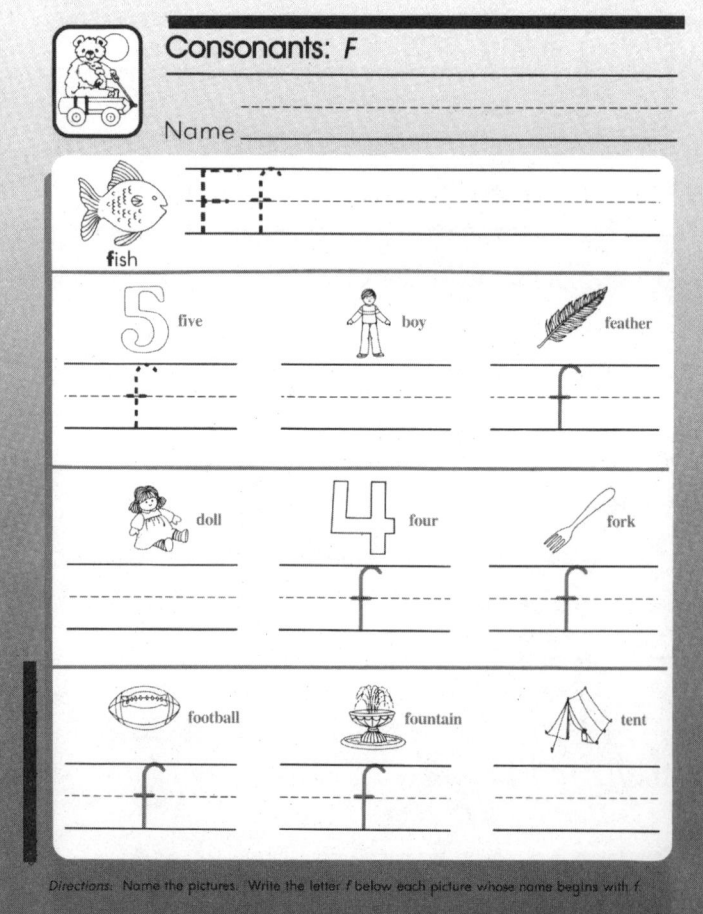
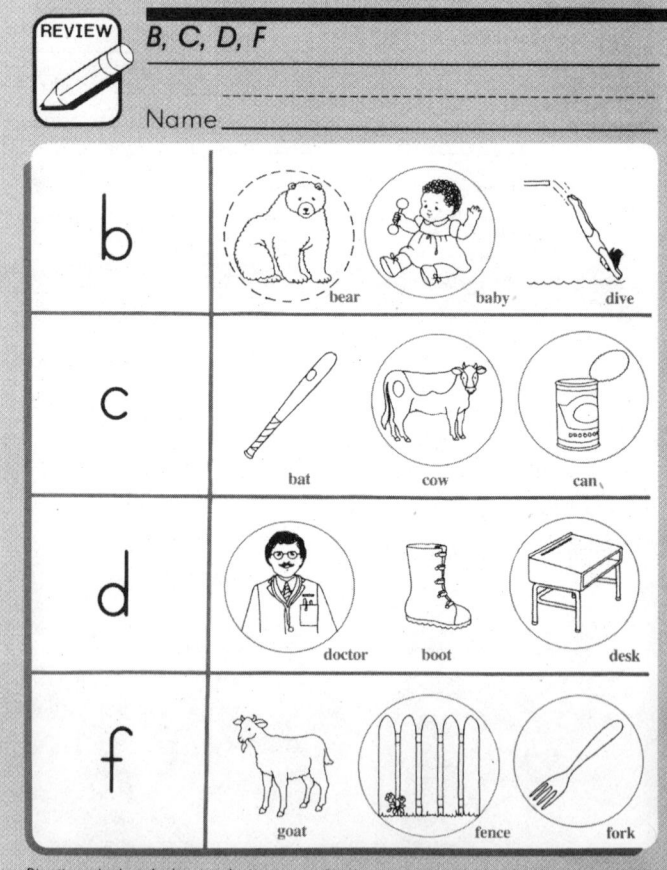

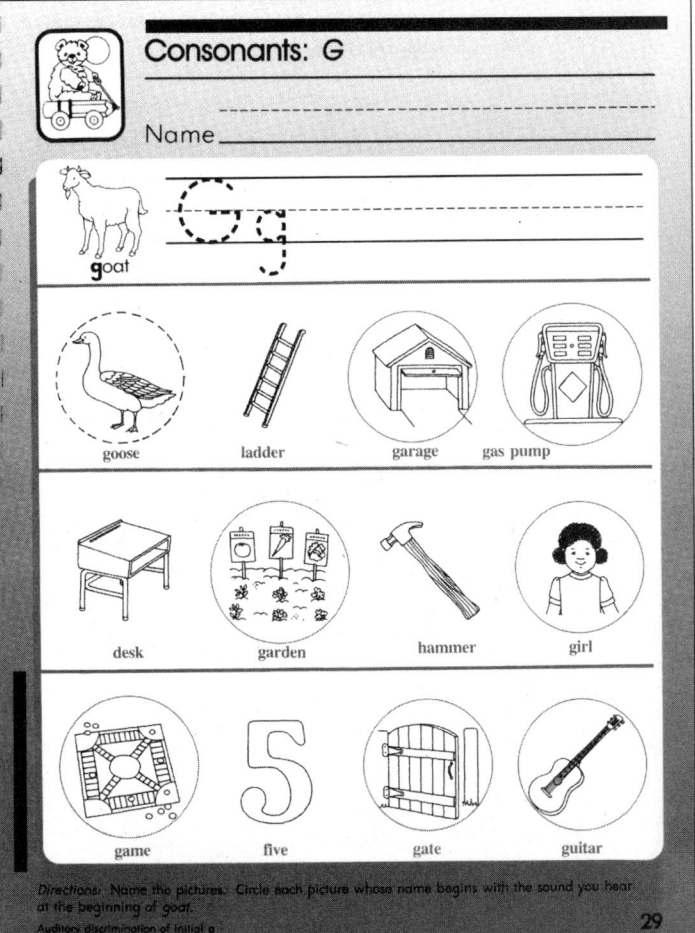
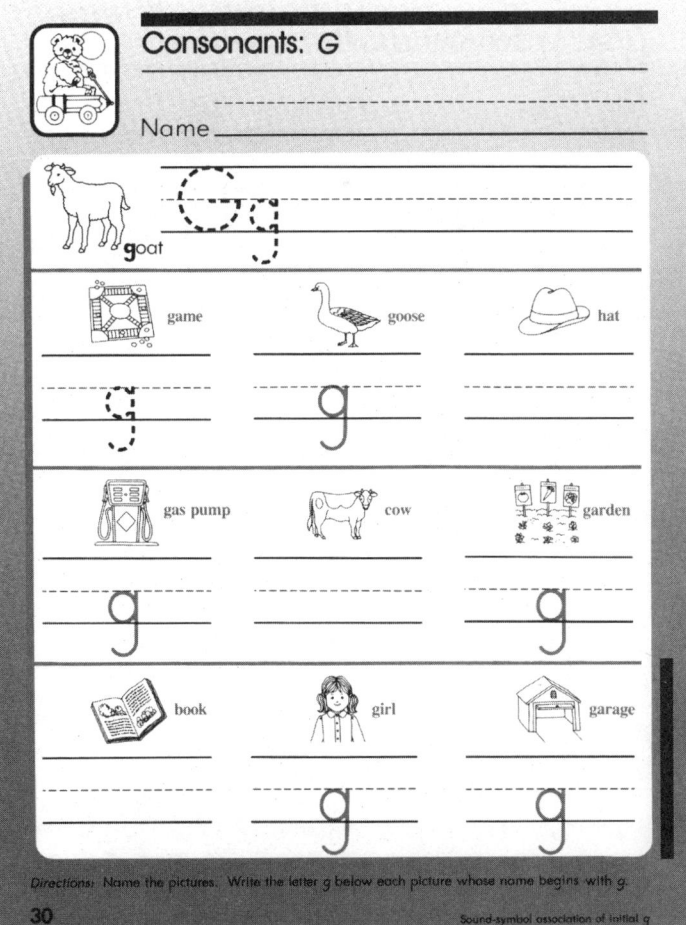

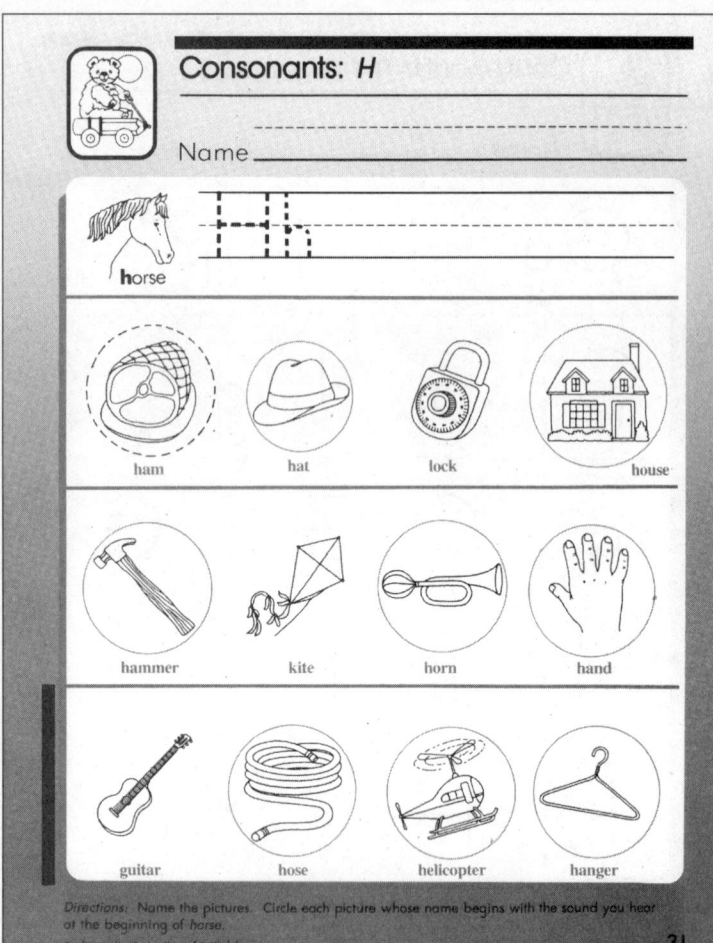
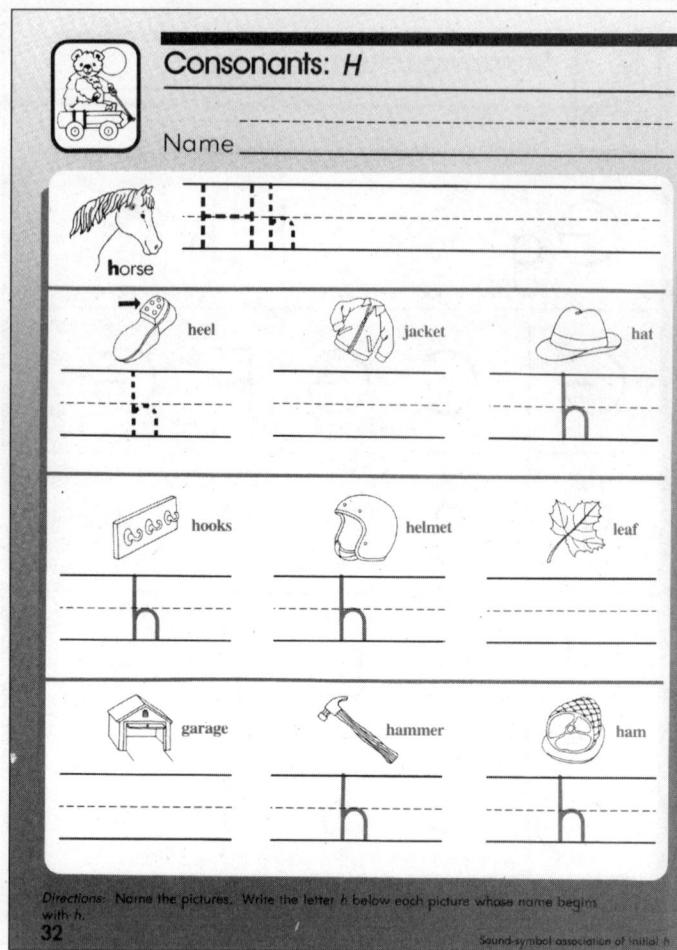

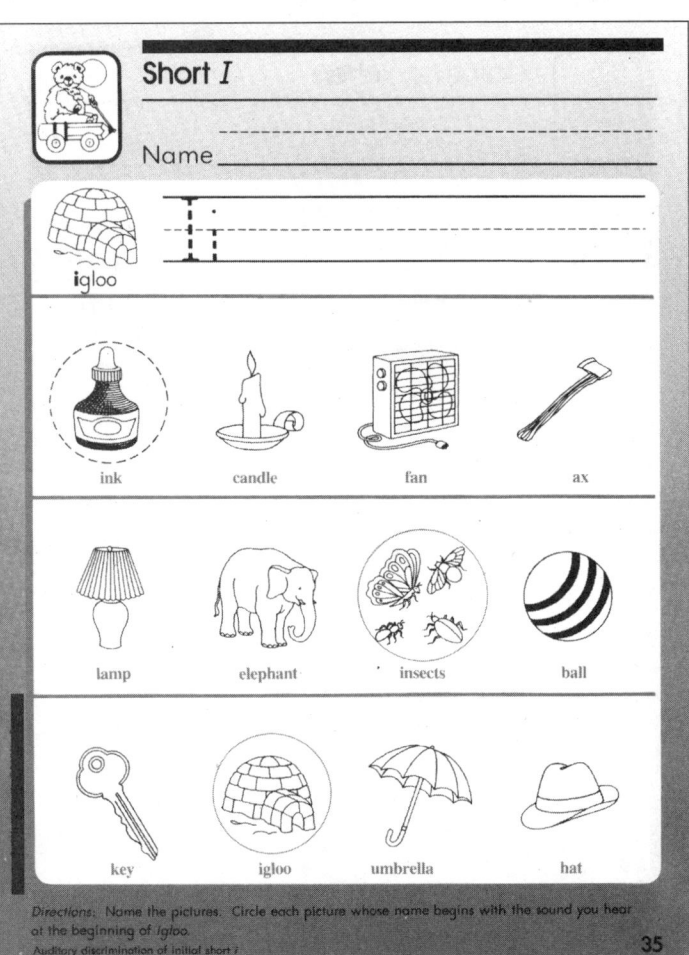
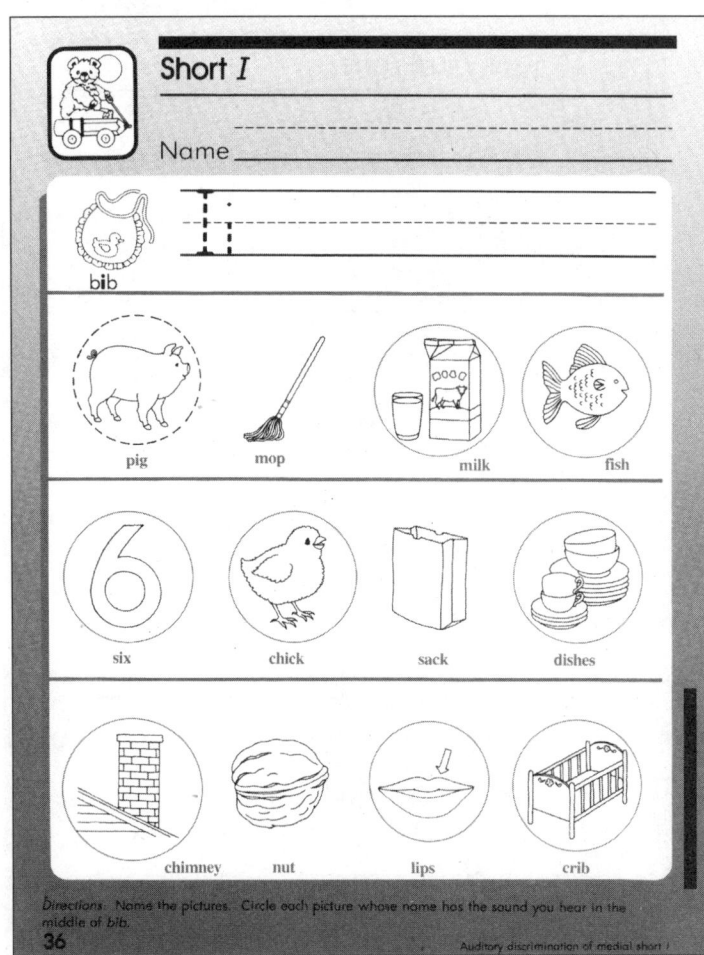
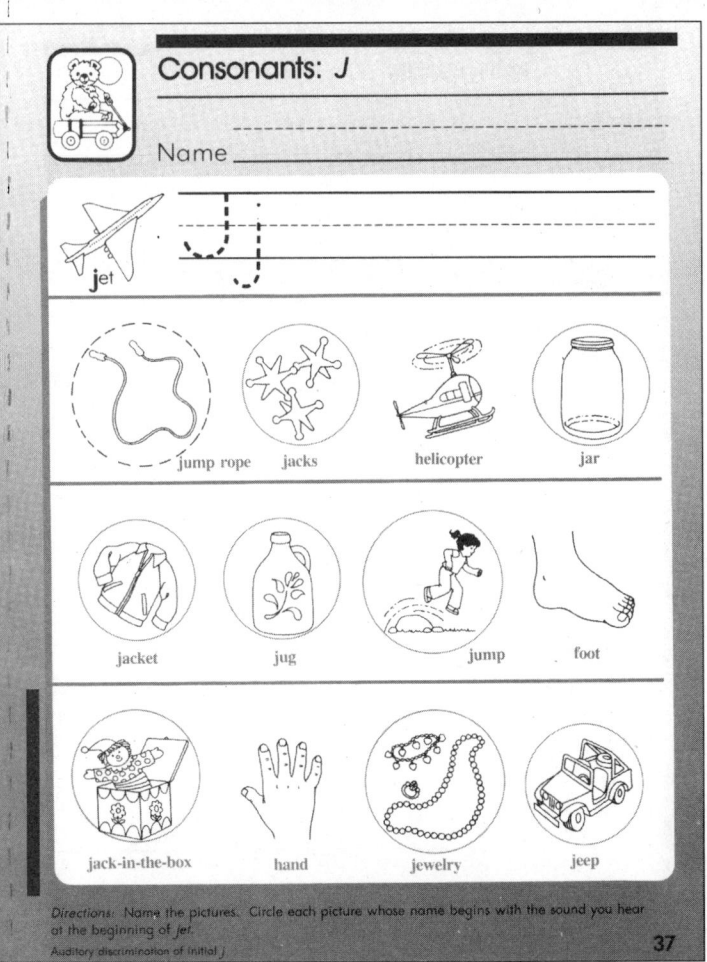
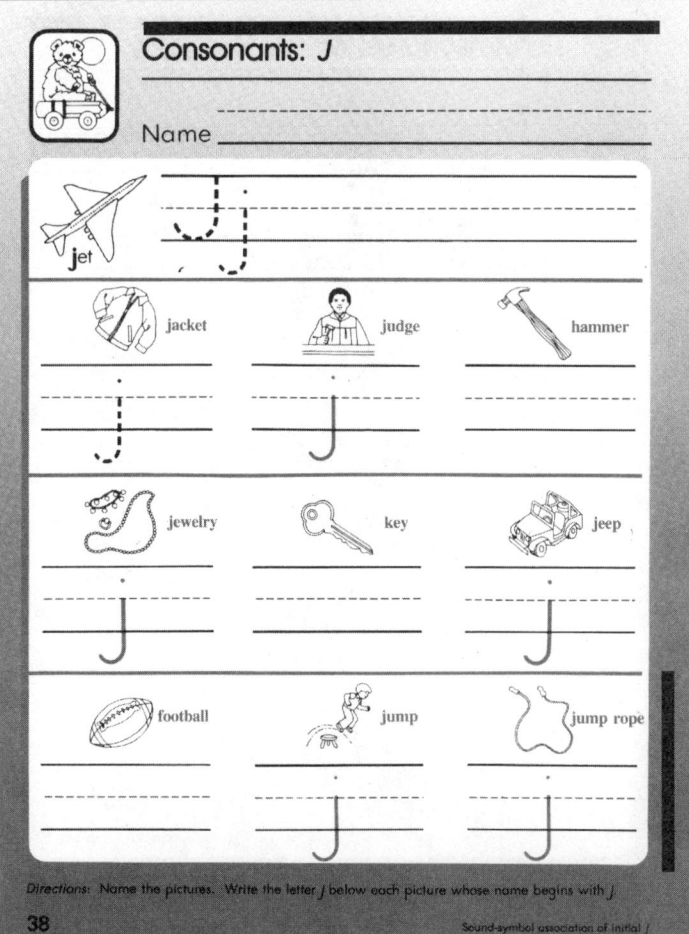

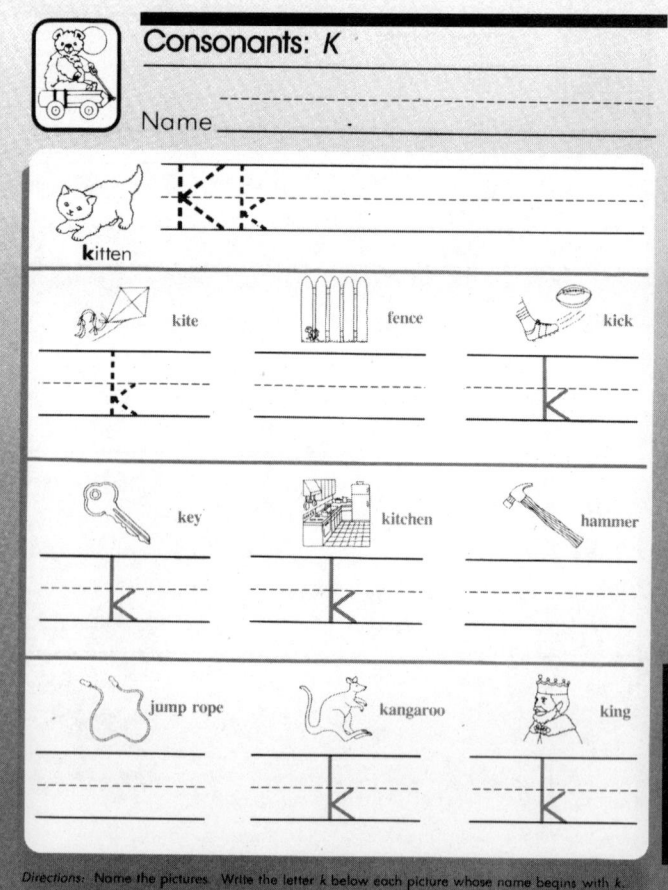

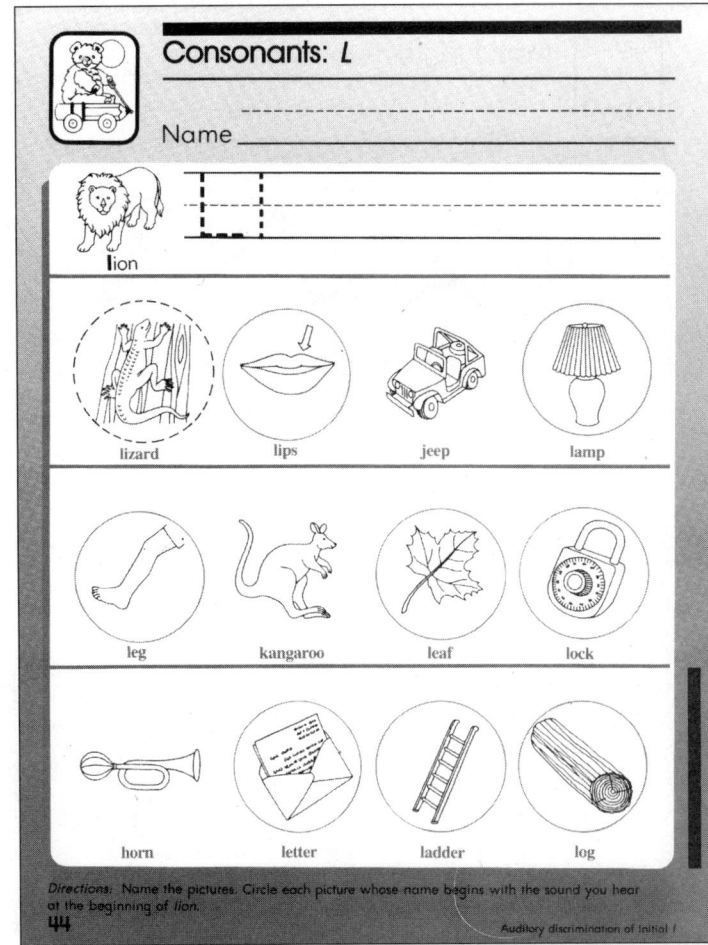
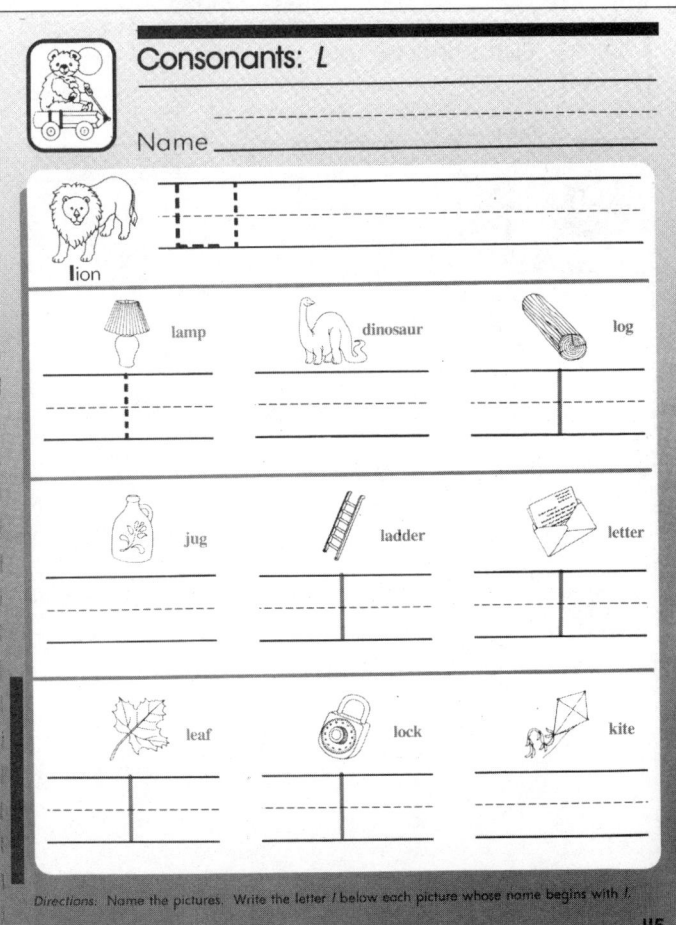

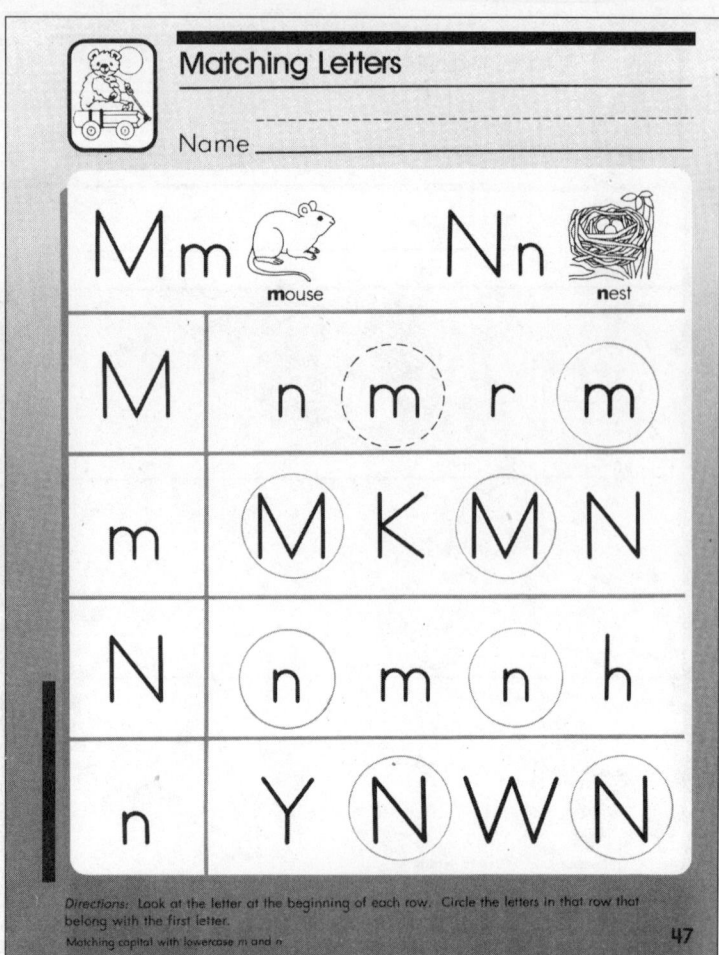
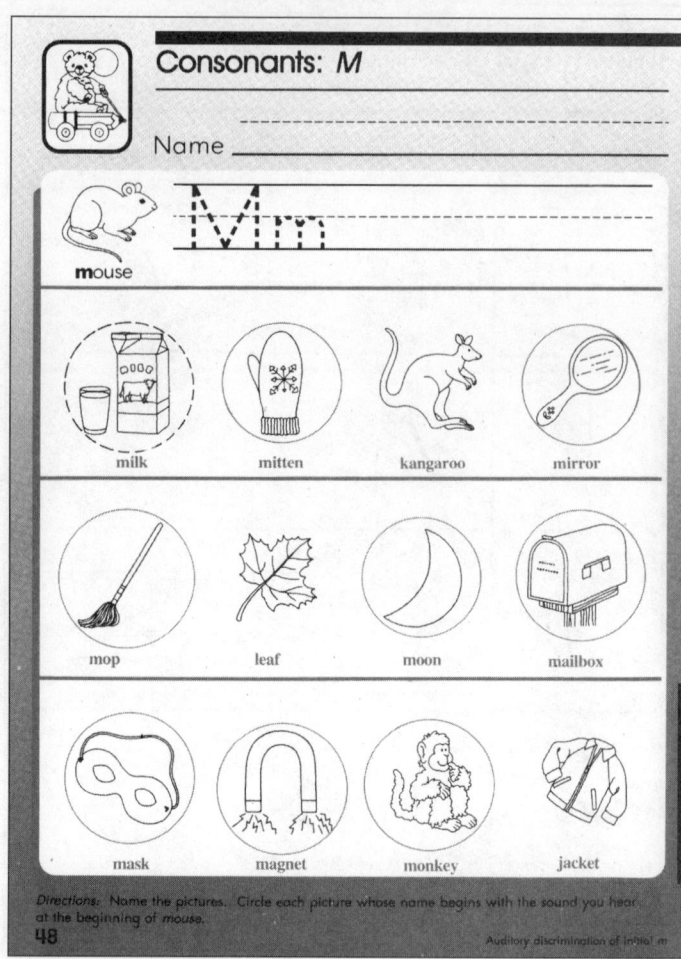

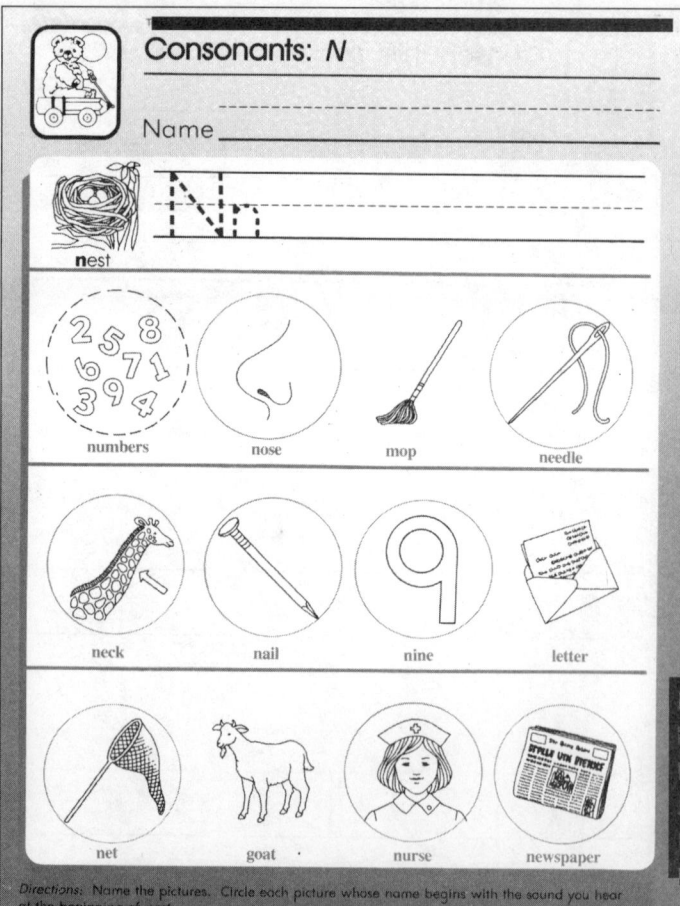

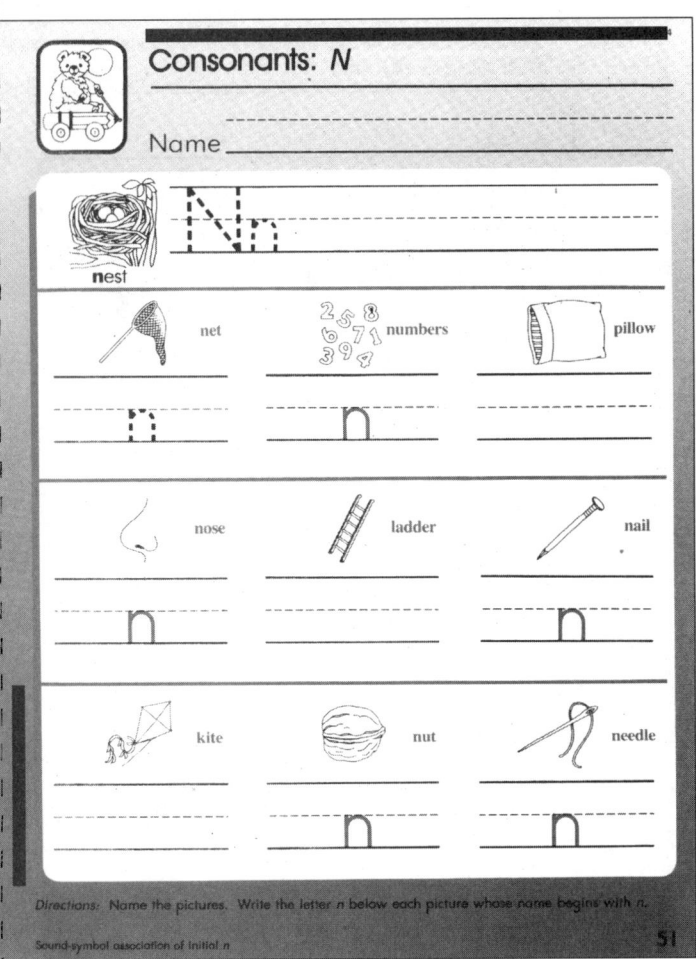
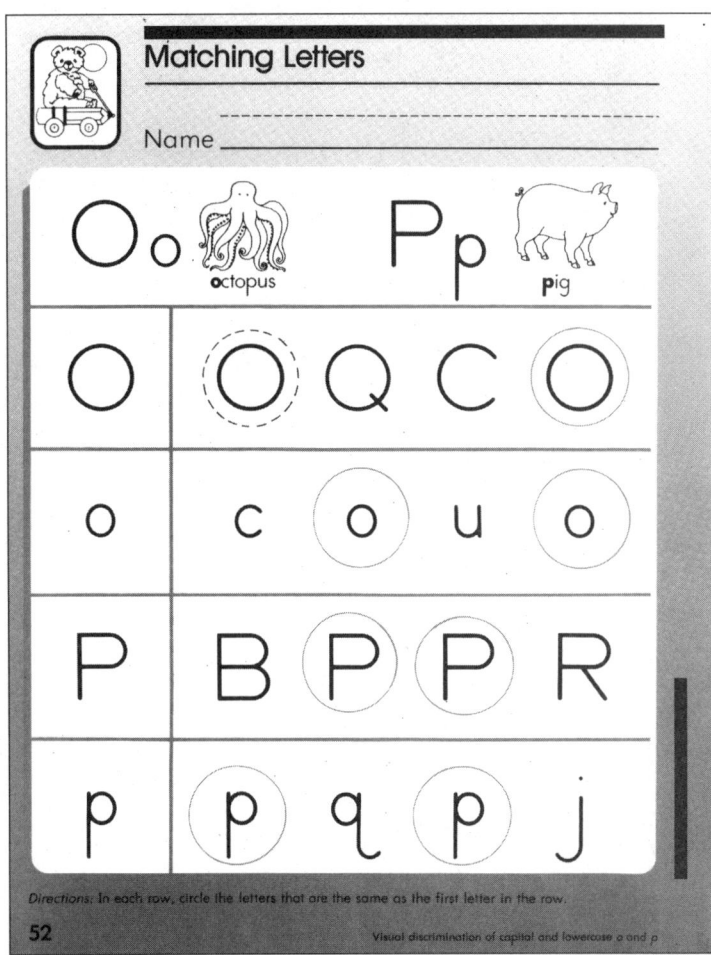

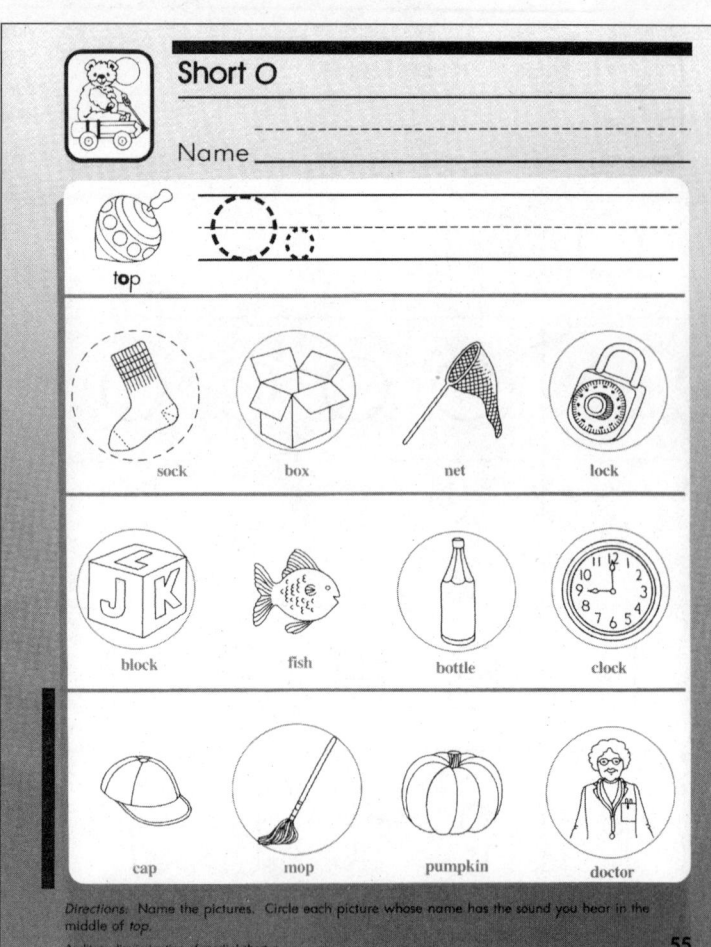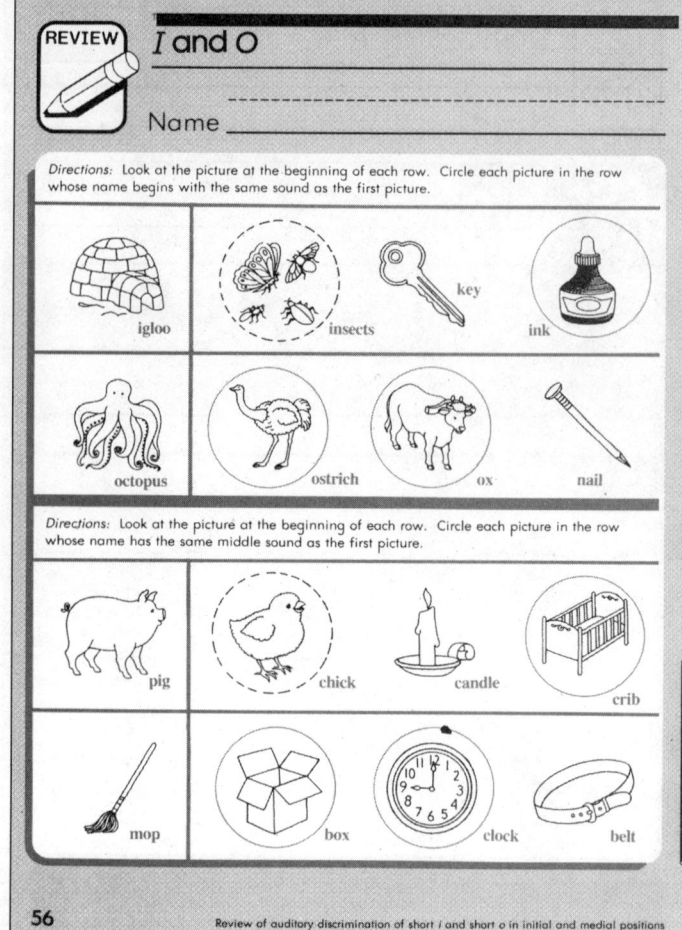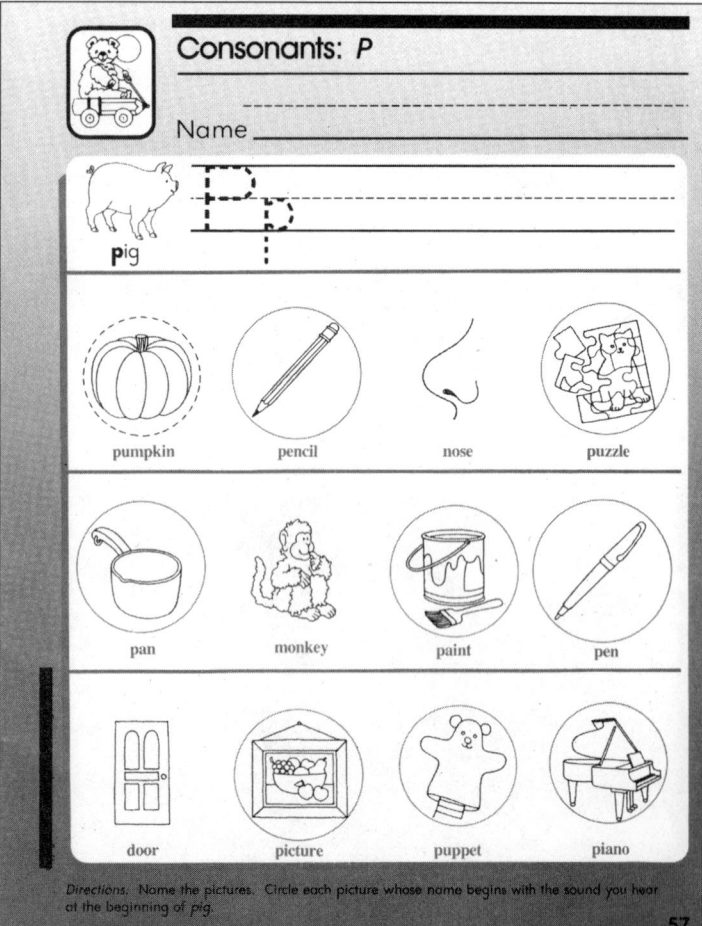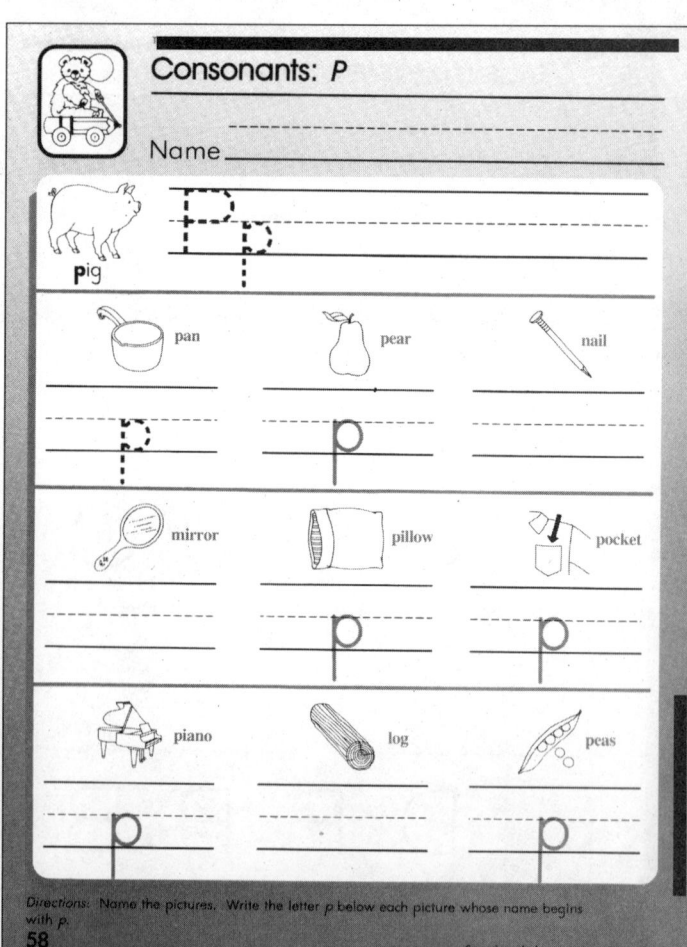

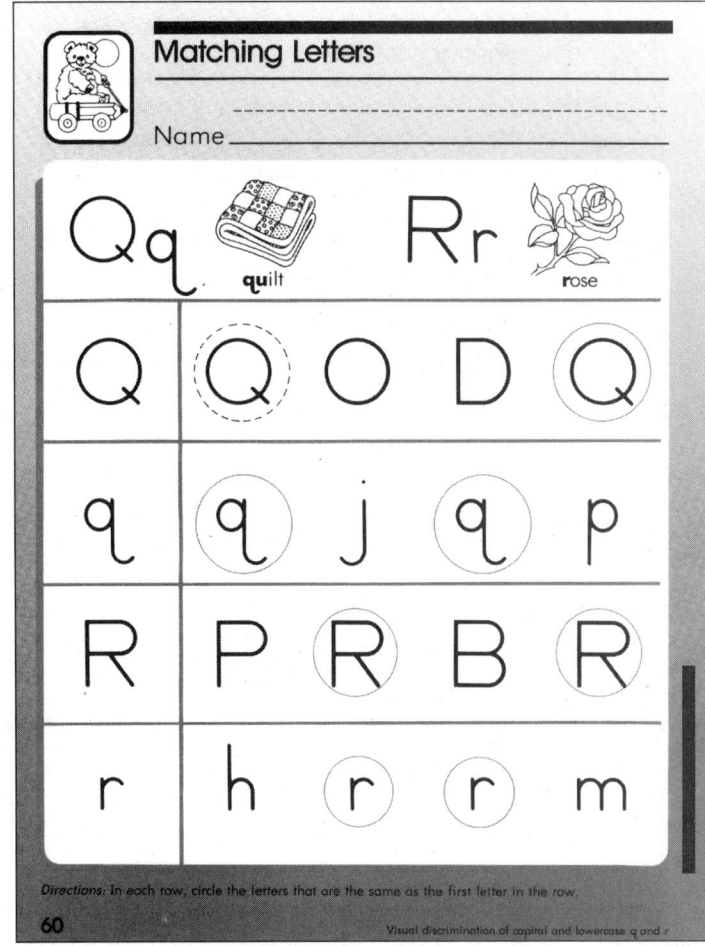
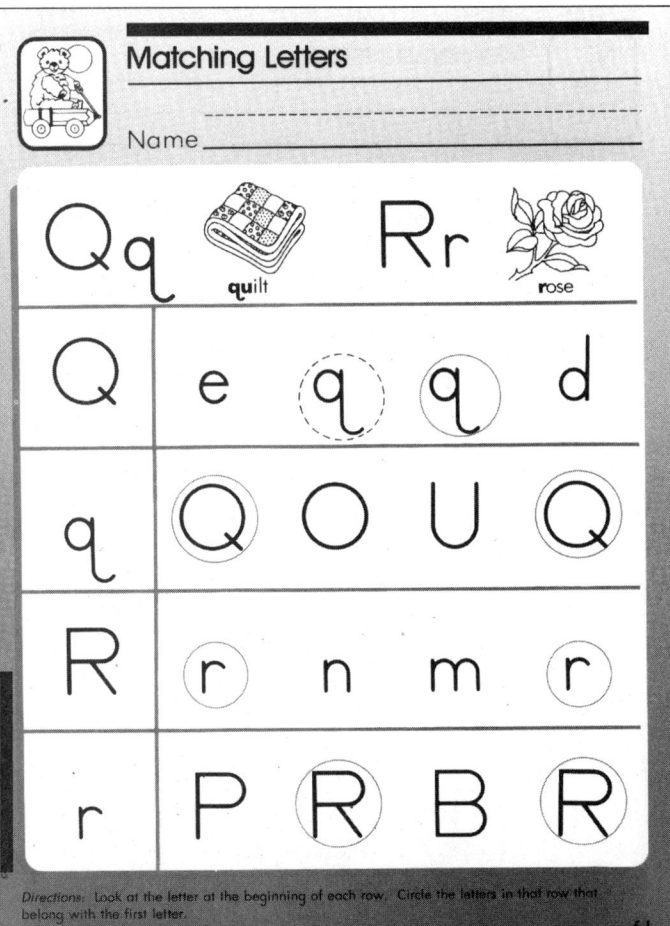

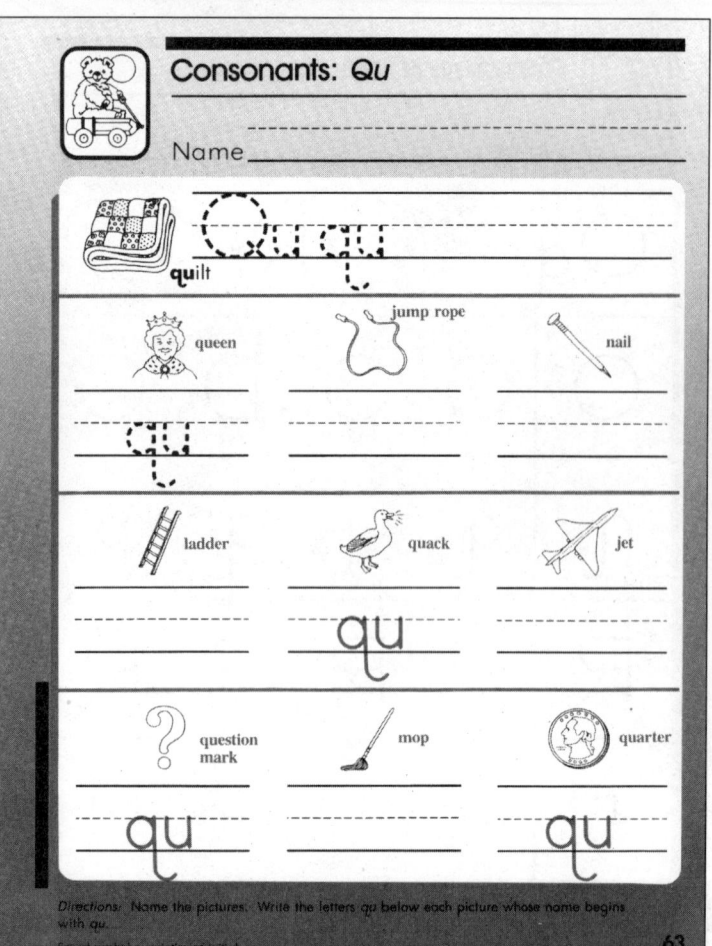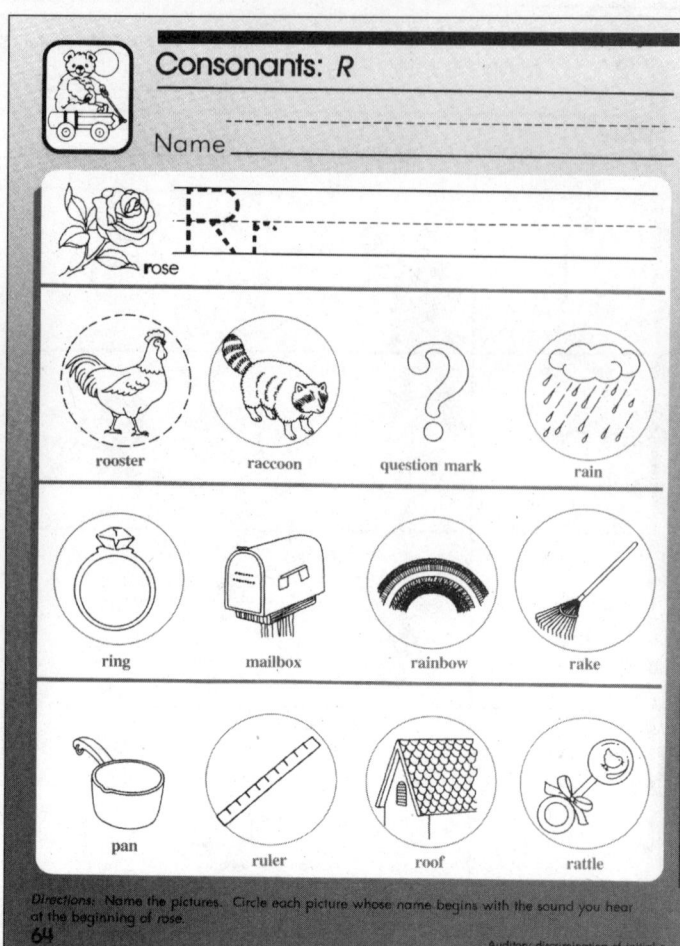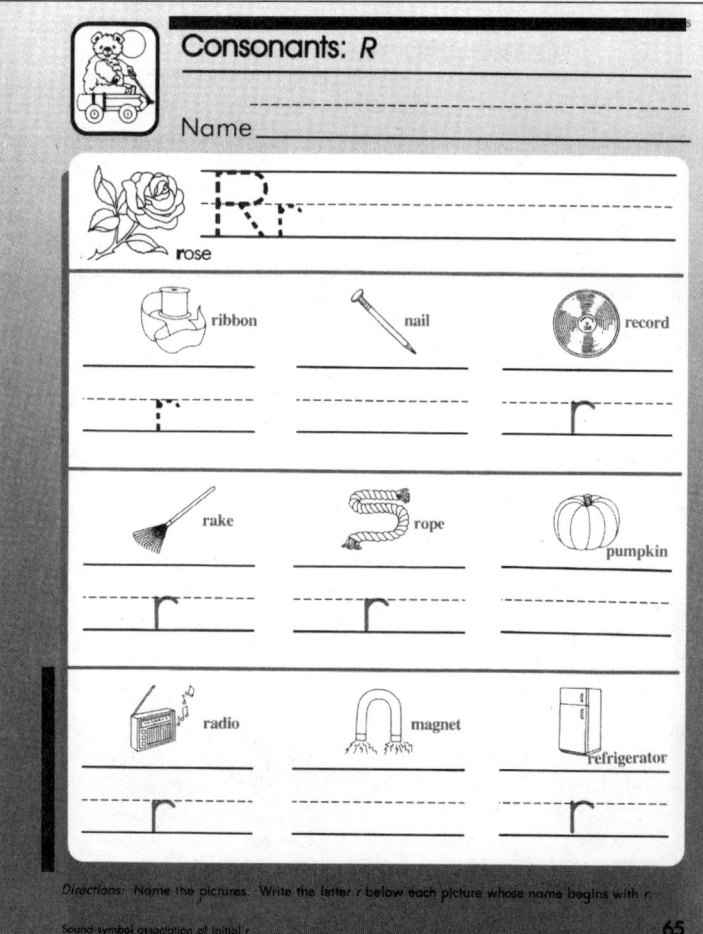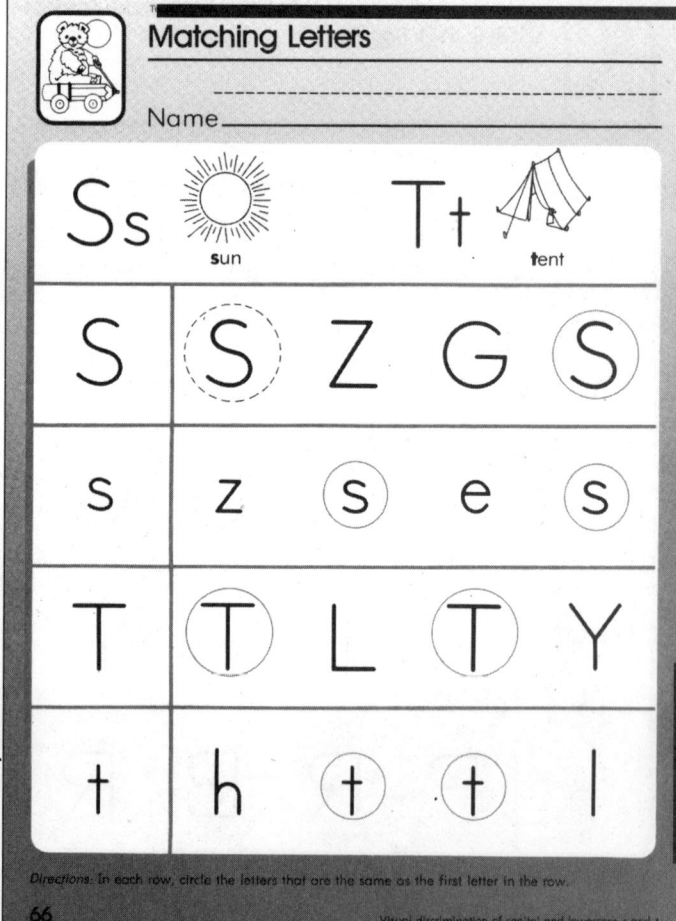

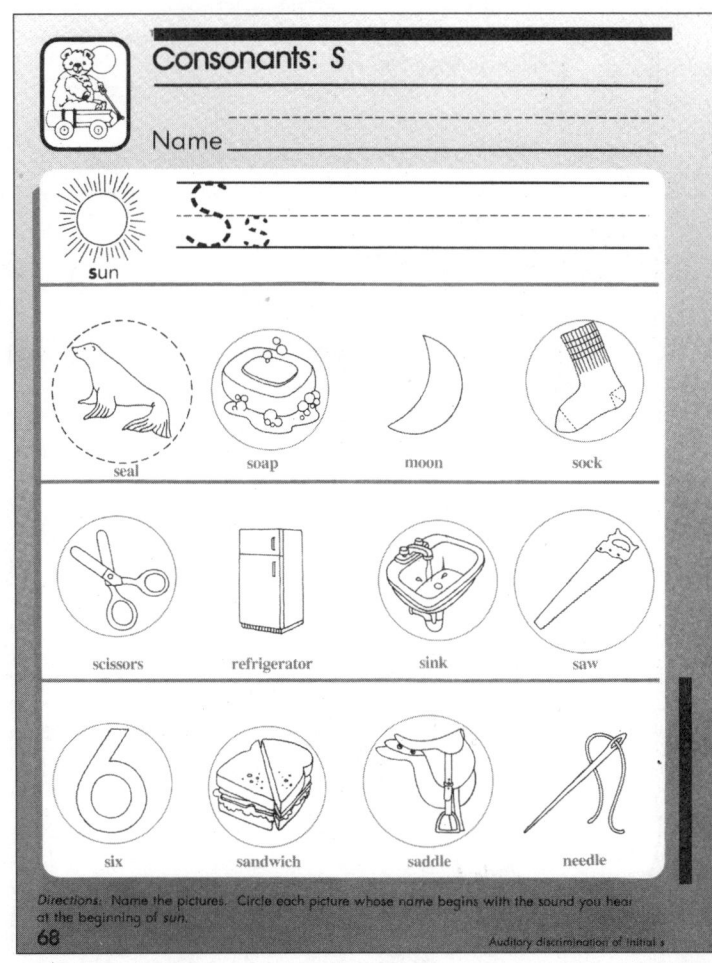
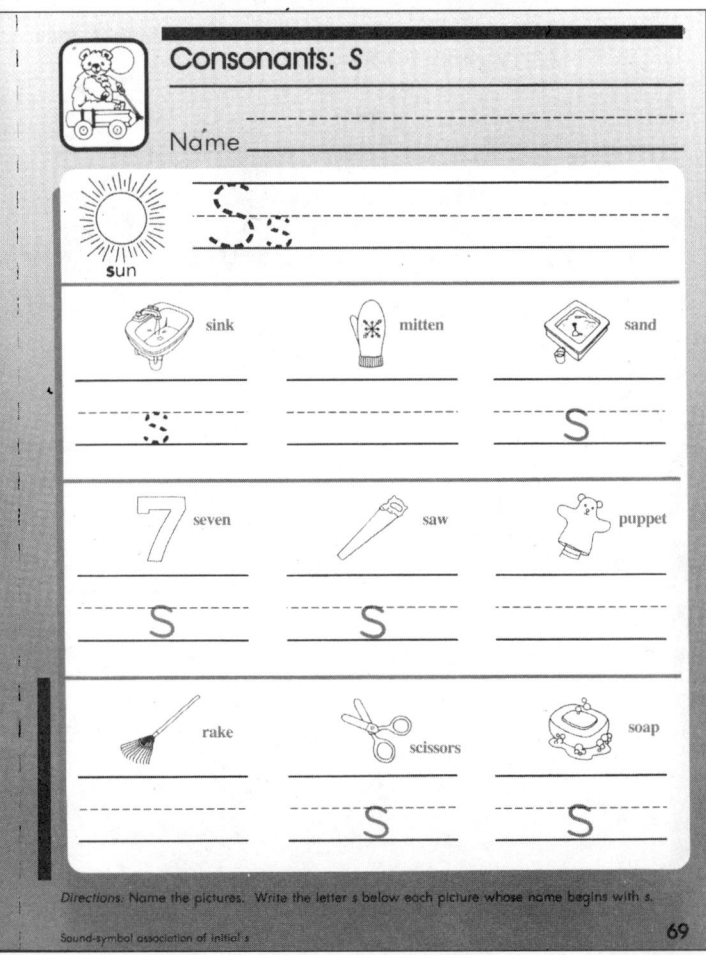
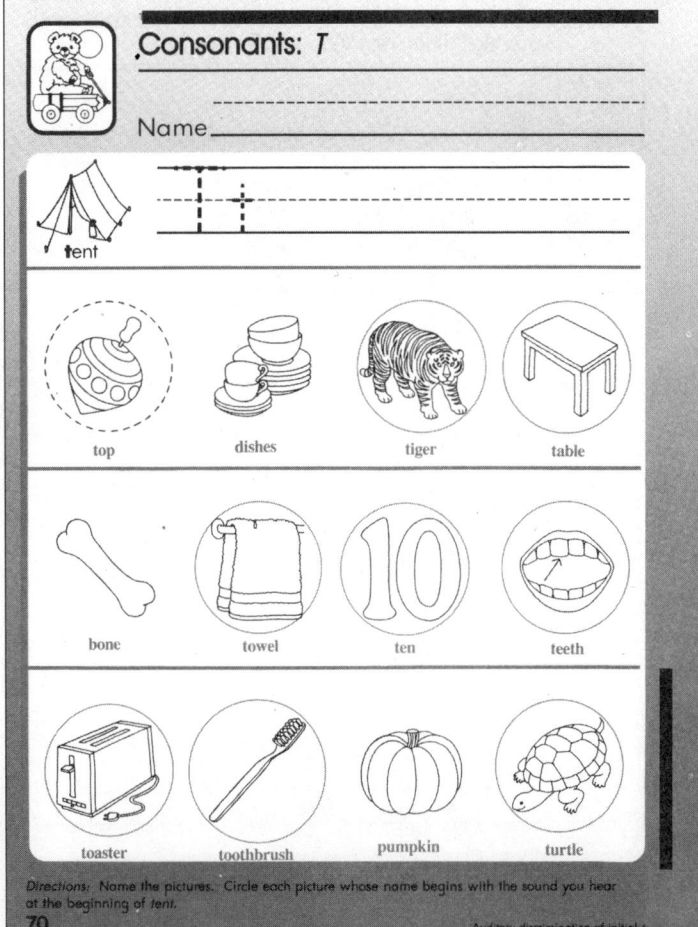

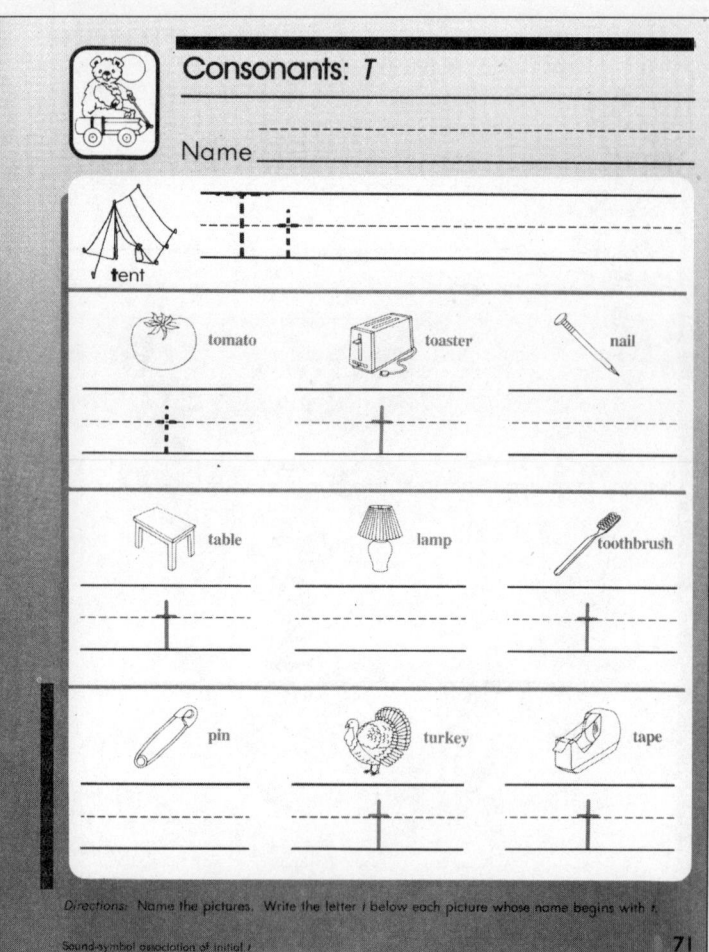
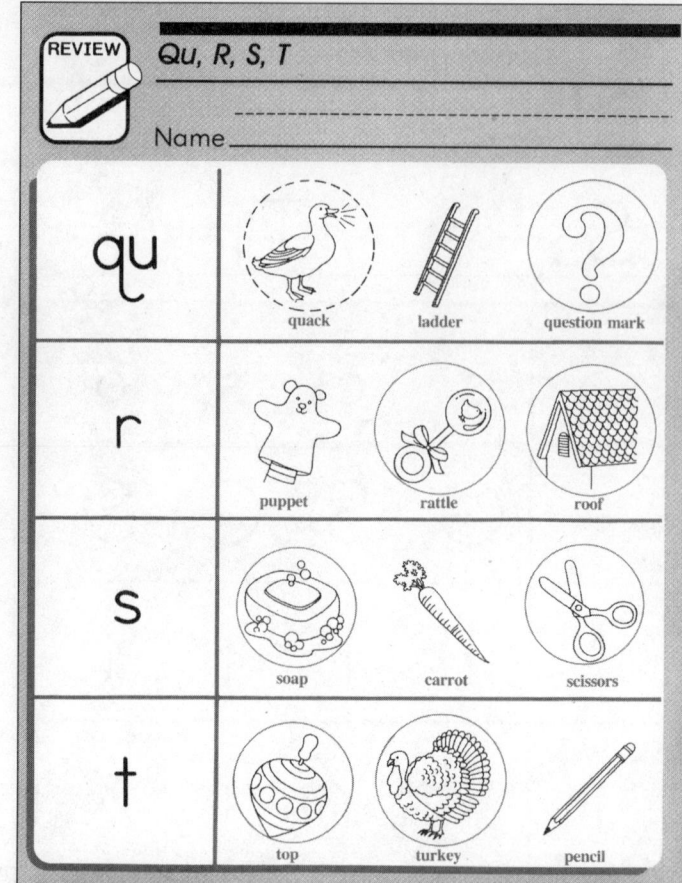

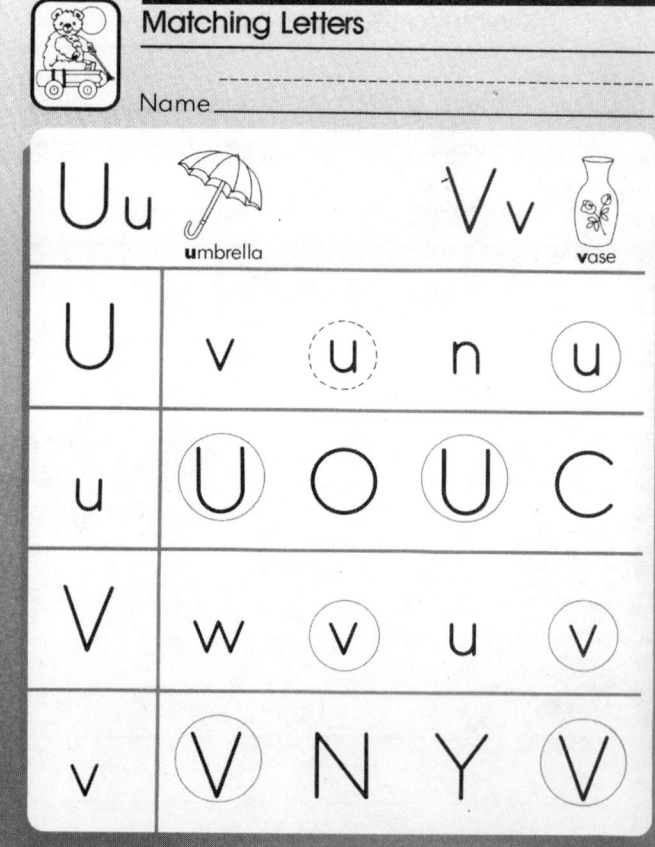

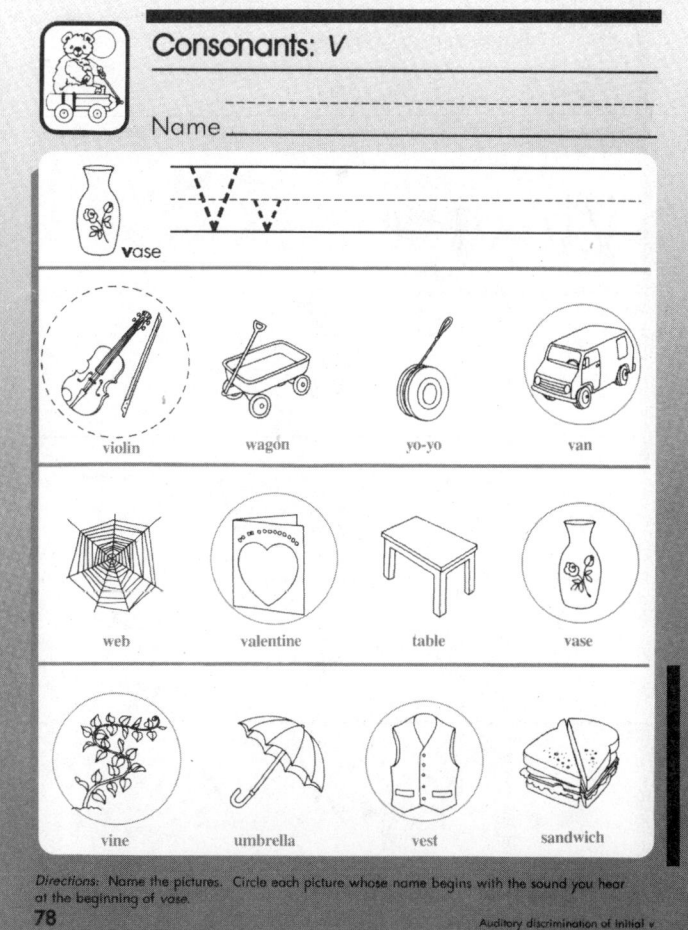

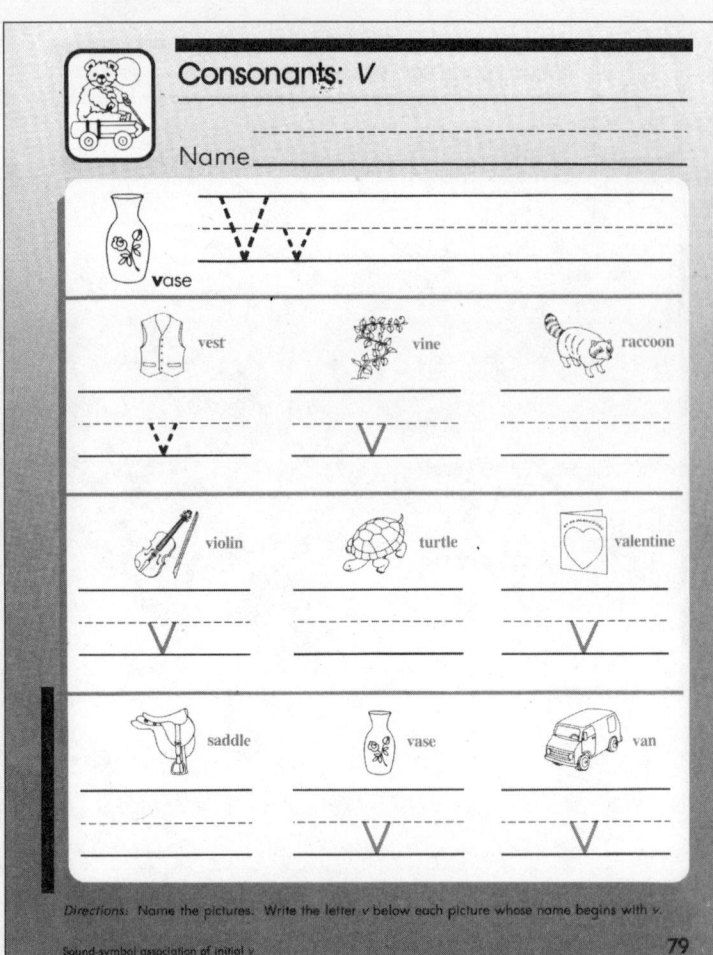
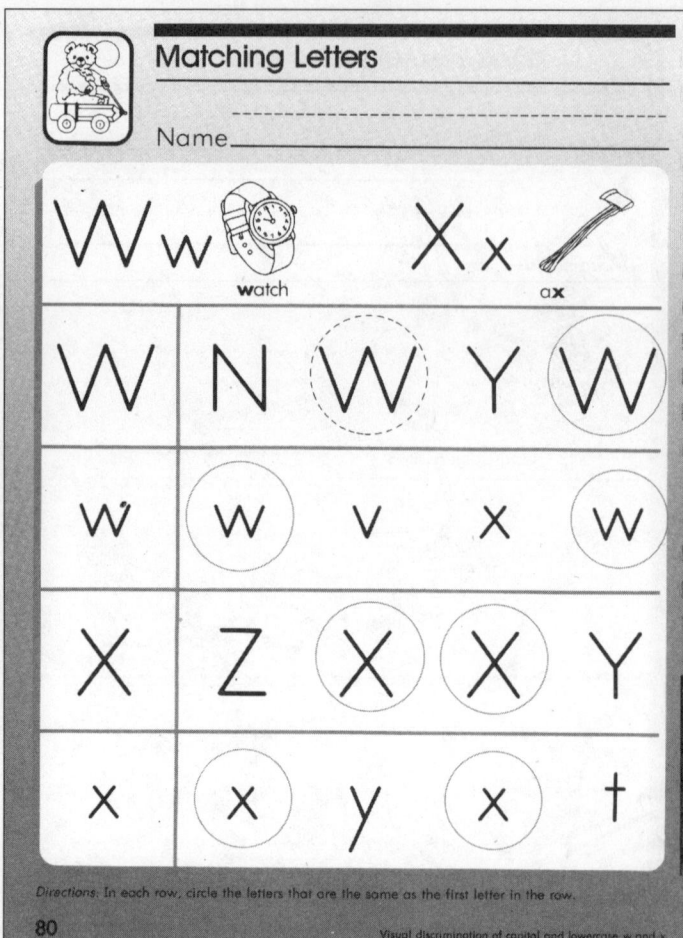
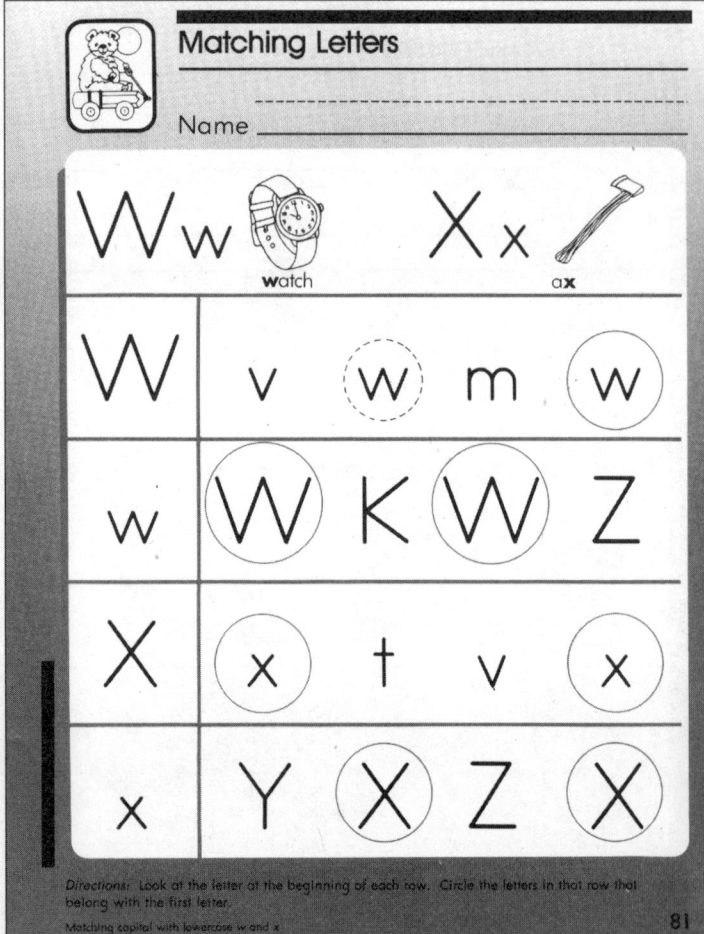
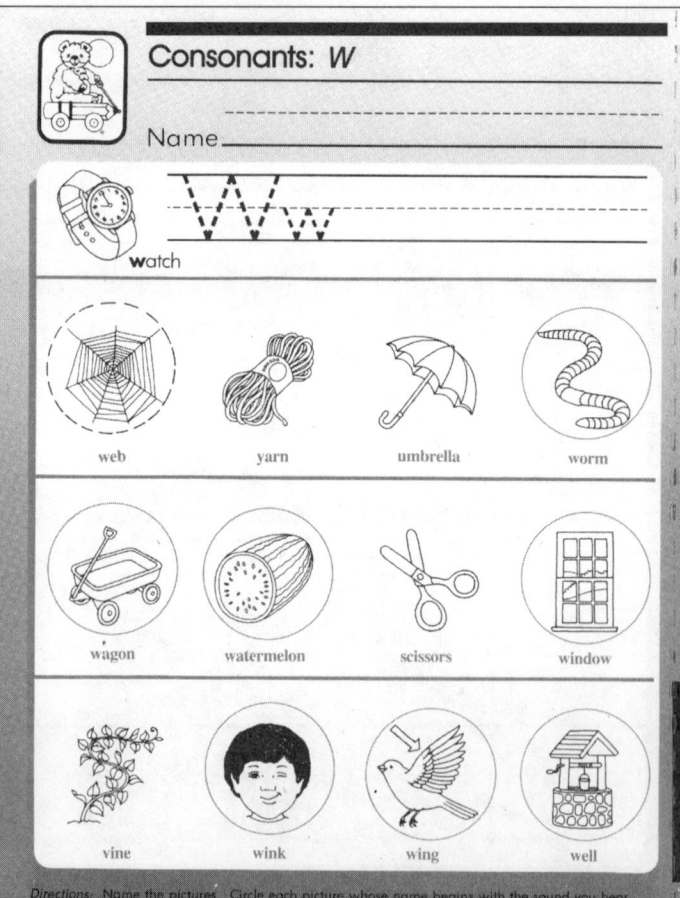

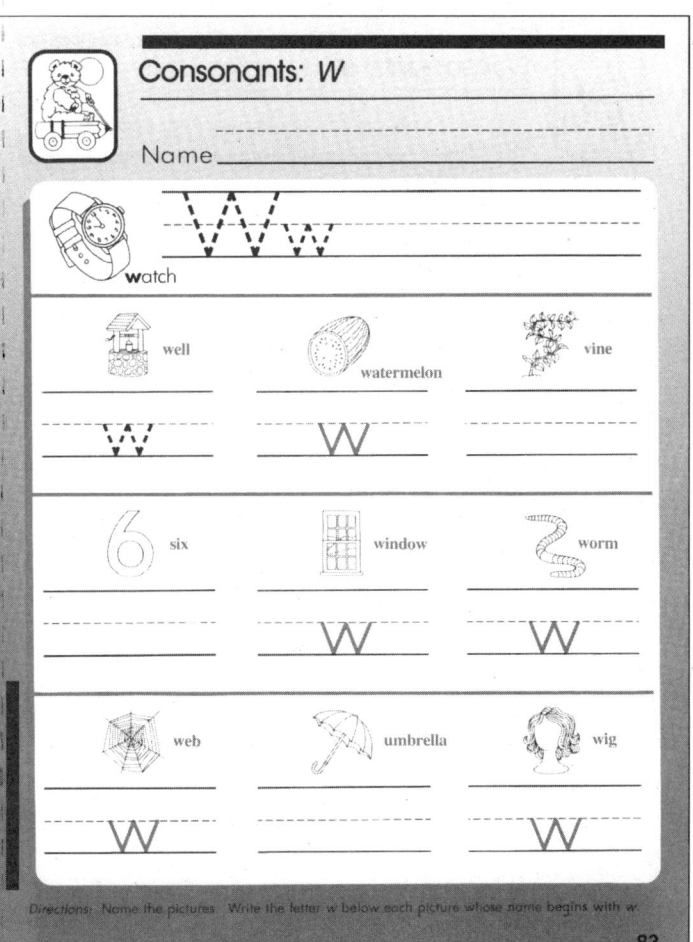

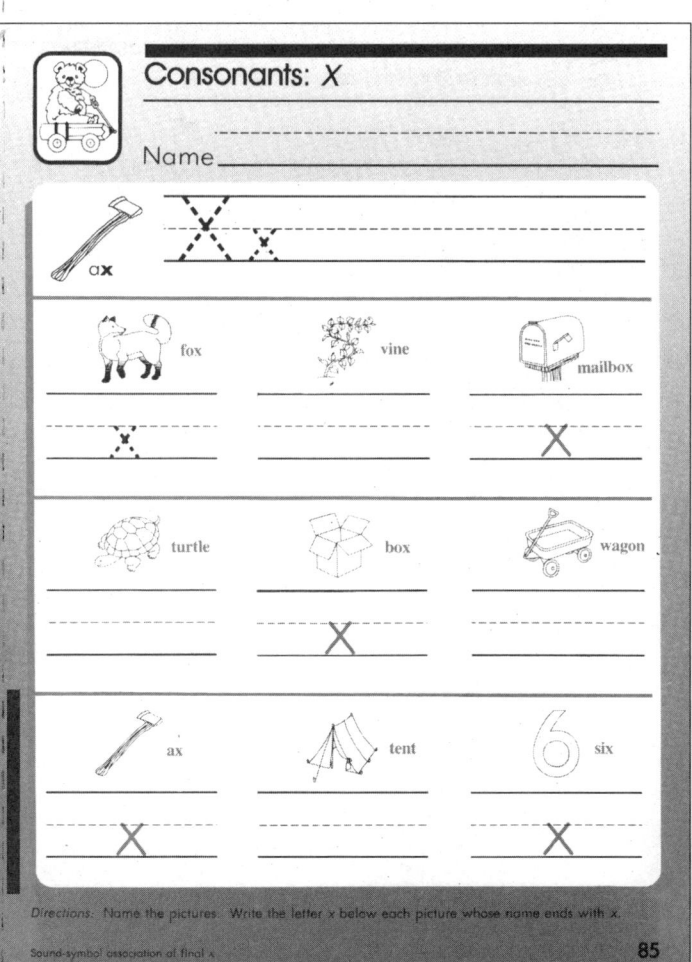

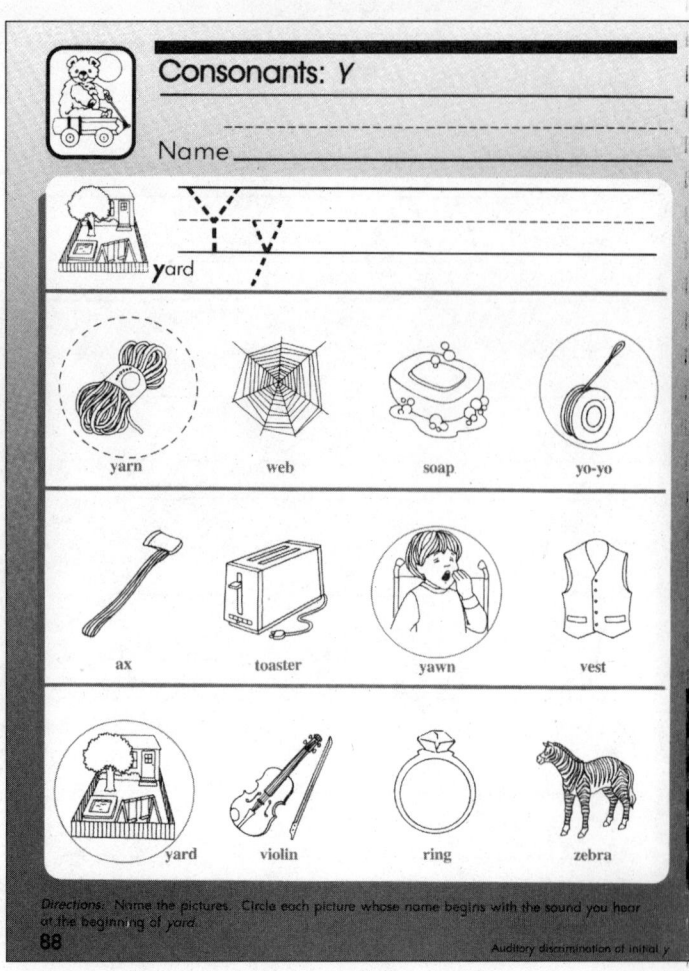
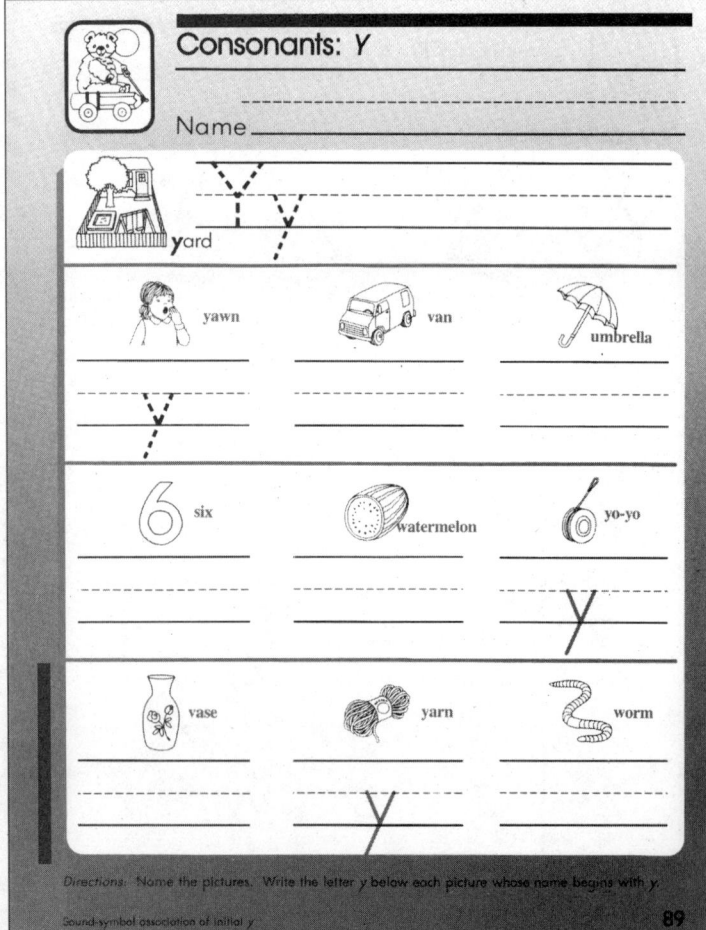
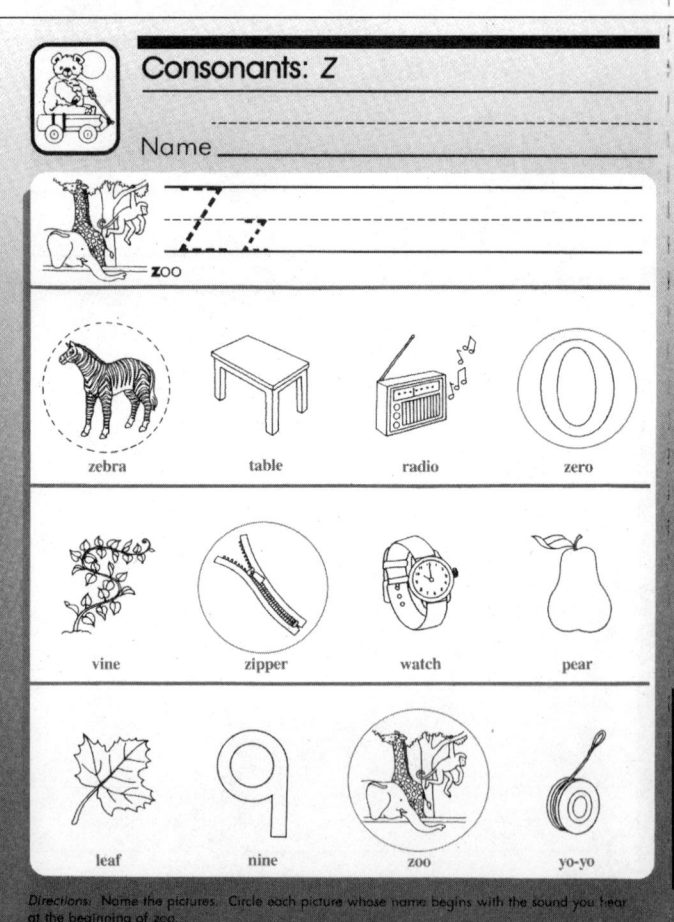

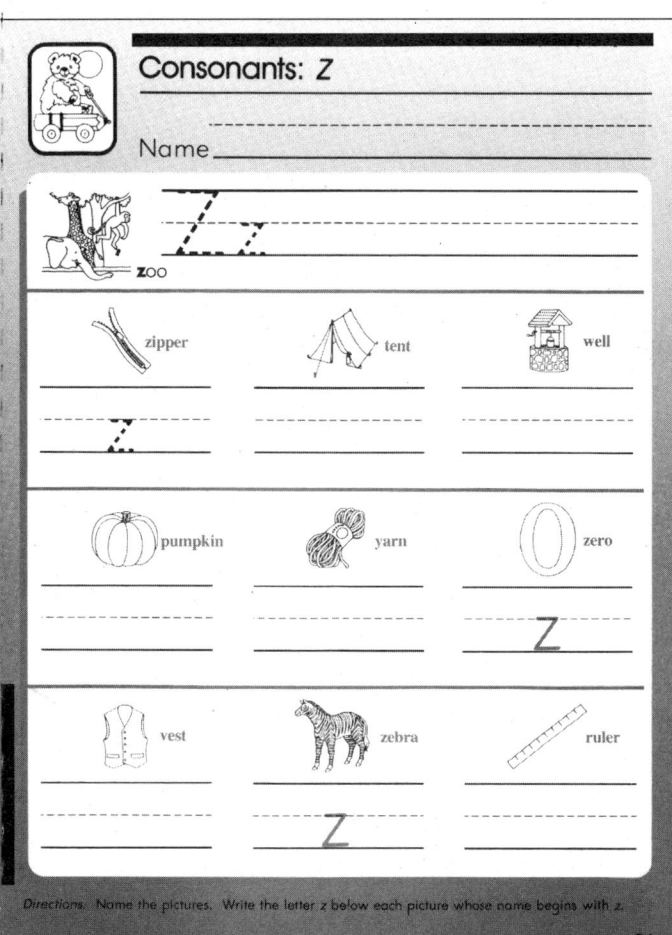
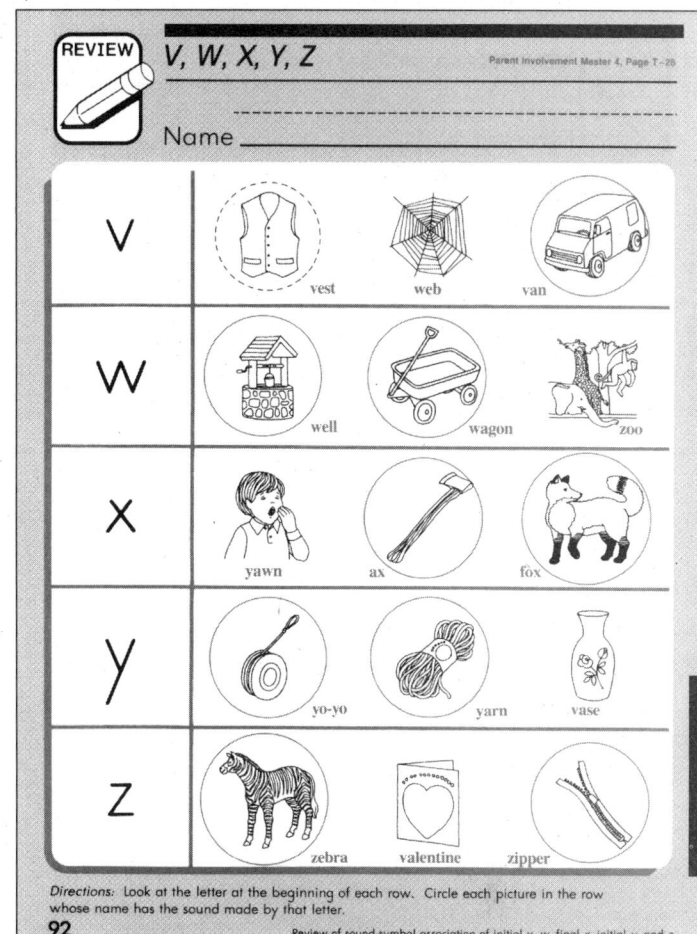
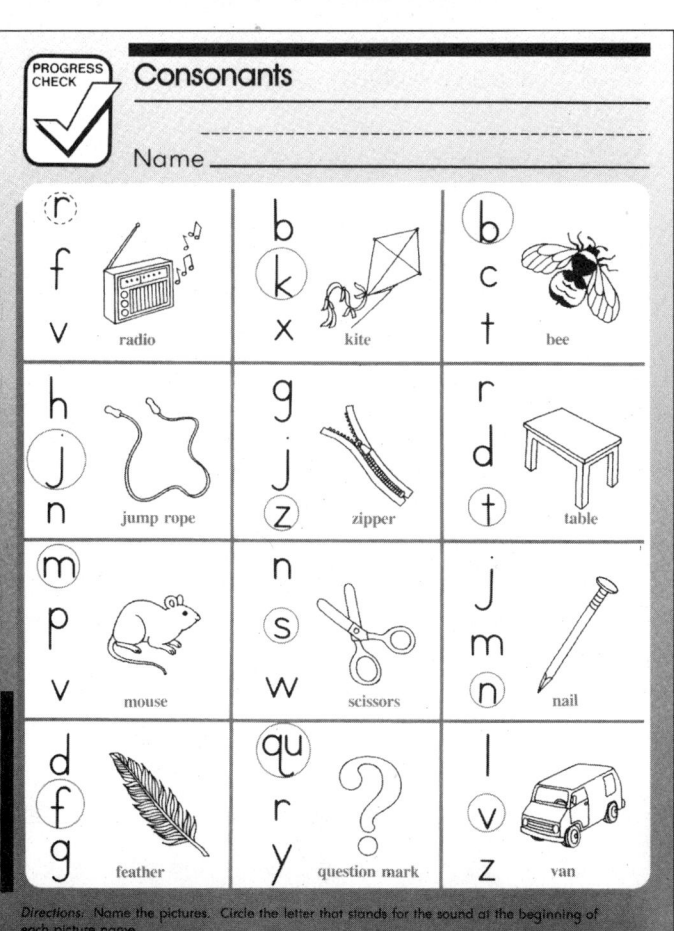
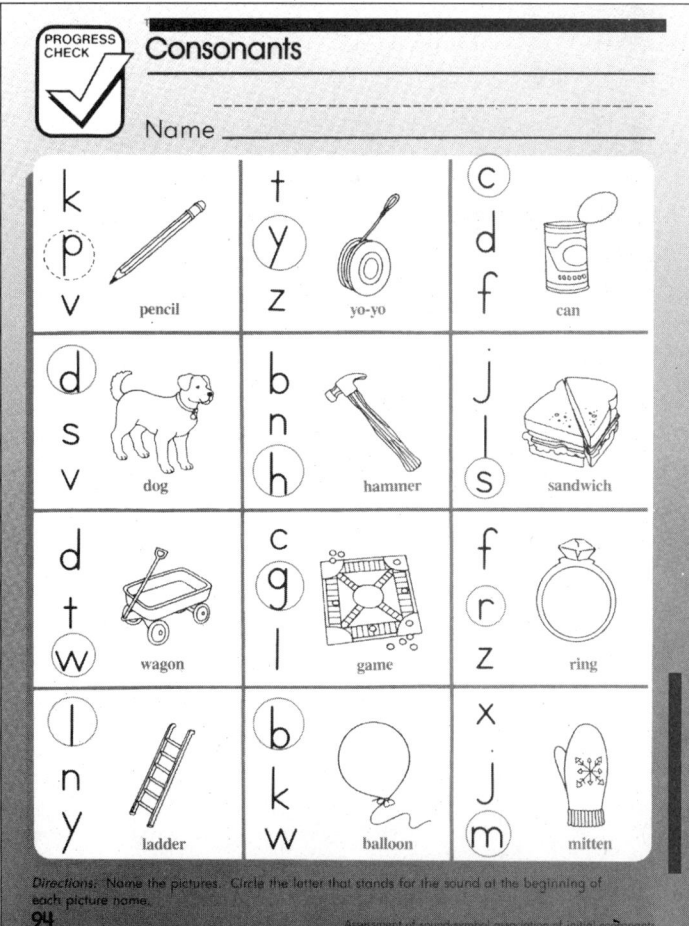

Vowels

PROGRESS CHECK ✓

Name _____

octopus	paint	ox	ostrich
egg	elephant	foot	elbow
umbrella	up	umpire	table
ant	bone	ax	alligator
igloo	insects	ink	hat

Directions: Name the first picture in each row. Then circle all the pictures in that row that begin with the same sound as the first picture.

Assessment of auditory discrimination of initial vowels